SPONSORSHIP PAGE

THIS BOOK IS SPONSORED BY

....

....

AS A GIFT TO

....

....

ON THIS DAY

....

'Each one must give as he has decided in his heart,
not reluctantly or under compulsion,
for God loves a cheerful giver.'
(2 Corinthians 9:7, ESV)

SCHOOL FOR IGBO HEBREW NATION AND PRAYER NETWORK

PRAYER M. MADUEKE

PRAYER PUBLICATIONS
UNITED STATES

© 2022 Prayer M. Madueke

ISBN: 979-8838264527

1st Edition

FREE EBOOKS

In order to say a 'Thank You' for purchasing *School for Igbo Hebrew Nation and Prayer Network*, I offer these books to you in appreciation.

> **[Click here](https://madueke.com/free-gift) or go to madueke.com/free-gift to download the eBooks now** <

Your testimonies will abound. <u>Click here</u> to see my other books. They have produced many testimonies and I want your testimony to be one too.

PRAYER REQUESTS OR COUNSELLING

Send me an email on <u>hello@madueke.com</u> if you need prayers or counselling or you have any questions.

MESSAGE FROM THE AUTHOR

PRAYER M. MADUEKE
CHRISTIAN AUTHOR

My name is Prayer Madueke, a spiritual warrior in the Lord's vineyard, an accomplished author, speaker, and expert on spiritual warfare and deliverance. I have published well over 100 books on every area of successful Christian living. I am an acclaimed family and relationship counselor with several titles dealing with critical areas in the lives of the children of God. I travel to several countries each year speaking and conducting deliverance sessions, breaking the yokes of demonic oppression and setting captives free.

It would be a delight to collaborate with you or your ministry in organized crusades, ceremonies, marriages and marriage seminars, special events, church ministration and fellowship for the advancement of God's kingdom here on earth.

You can find all my books on my webstore: store.madueke.com

Feel free to visit my website madueke.com for devotionals and other materials. God bless you.

TABLE OF CONTENTS

CHAPTER 1

VISION FOR THE IGBO NATION

- To raise a prayer team that will be committed to pray for the liberation of Igbo nation.

- To pray and destroy the ancestral and imported altars of the devil in Igbo land.

- To build an altar, a camp ground, where every Igbo and people from other nations of the world will gather for prayer.

THE ORIGINALITY OF THE IGBO NATION

- To pray for Igbo ministers' liberation and empowerment with the 9 fruits and gifts of the Spirit.

- To pray and encourage the Igbo to invest in their land until Igbo land is developed and becomes the market place of Africa/World.

- To pray and make Igbo land the centre of academic excellence and the pride of Africa in every aspect.

- To prepare the Igbo for the rapture of the saints and the second coming of Christ, and to partake in the end time revival.

- To restore back the lost glory of Igbo race in Africa.

> "Gad, a troop shall overcome him: but he shall overcome at the last."
>
> — (GENESIS 49:19)
>
> Jesus saw Nathanael coming to him, and saith of him, behold an Israelite indeed, in whom is no guile!"
>
> — (JOHN 1:47)

THE ORIGINAL IGBO BORN

- Igbo are known everywhere from the beginning to be intelligent, industrious, and to quality decision and standard set by God (Daniel 1:8).

As outlined in (Hebrew 11:24-29), the Igbo follow through each verse:

- (Hebrews 11:24) By faith Moses, when he was come to years, refused to be called the son of Pharaoh's daughter;

- (Hebrews 11:25) Choosing rather to suffer affliction with the people of God, than to enjoy the pleasures of sin for a season;

- (Hebrews 11:26) esteeming the reproach of Christ greater riches than the treasures in Egypt: for he had respect unto the recompense of the reward.

- (Hebrews 11:27) by faith, he forsook Egypt, not fearing the wrath of the king: for he endured, as seeing him who is invisible.

- (Hebrews 11:28) through faith, he kept the Passover, and the sprinkling of blood, lest he that destroyed the firstborn should touch them.

- (Hebrews 11:29) by faith, they passed through the Red sea as by dry land, which the Egyptians assaying to do were drowned.

- **Esteem** (consider, measure, judge, and regard before forming opinion).

- **Refuse** (after considering the various sides, refuse and will reject to do wrong).

- **Choose** (chose in favor of eternal realities; go for lasting riches).

- **Forsake** (take definite action on decisions reached in steps 1, 2, 3).

- **Endure** (Igbo never allow circumstances to hinder their progress; they are determined to end well).

- **Keep** (They keep what they already know is instructed by God in His word and never compromise).

- **Pass through** (They follow through, going all the way across the uncross-able to please God).

7 QUALITIES OF ORIGINAL IGBO PERSON

- They are not ashamed in doing what they believe is right; they are bold in righteousness (Daniel 1:8; 2 Timothy 1:7; Hebrews 13:6; Philippians 1:27, 28).

- Their standard is uncommon (Daniel 1:8, 12; Philippians 3:7-11; 2 Timothy 1:14).

- They seek for divine protection, so they believe in God in the midst of earthly enemies (Daniel 1:9; Colossians 3:1-4; 2 Corinthians 1:8-10; Revelation 3:8-10).

- They are goal getters and do not quit in the midst of oppositions. They move with unhindered persistence. (Daniel 1:10-12; Exodus 5:1, 2; 6:10, 11; 7:10-13; 8:25-32; 10:8-11; 12:30-36).

- A closed door is nothing to an original Igbo person. When an Igbo man makes up his mind, he moves with firm principle.

- They have faith only in God; they face every challenge with unblemished faith in God (Daniel 1:12, 13; Genesis 28:15; 1 Samuel 12:22; Psalm 9:10; 25:10; Isaiah 42:16; Hebrews 10:24).

- An original Igbo person hates sin and fights with the last drop of his blood to overcome sin.

■ Sin brings doubt, but purity brings confidence. If the heart is pure, faith is strong. No matter who gets angry for your uncompromising standard or stand, if you take your stand with God's word, God will stand by you. If you resolve on the right, people will soon find that God has gone ahead to prepare the way.

■ Their confidence in God is absolute, that is why their persecutions, trials and tests are always unusual (Daniel 1:14-16; Nehemiah 2:4-8; Matthew 10:18-20; Romans 8:14).

Let us propose what we want from God and from the nation like Daniel did in the exercise of faith, through prayers and not by fighting carnally Genesis 27:40, 41; Esther 4:15-16.

■ Igbo are great achievers. They enjoy immeasurable blessings everywhere they are because the God of Abraham is their God (Daniel 1:17-21; Exodus 15:26; 23:22; Deuteronomy 4:40; 15:4, 5; Job 36:11; John 14:23; 15:6, 7; Hebrews 10:36).

■ Your blessing depends on your total commitment to God. Physical health, vigor, intellectual attainment, strength, moral and spiritual power are words associated with every true Igbo person. In addition; continuous prosperity and influence came on the original Igbo people, and Daniel for their uncompromising stand and faith in God.

■ We can compare the Igbo in Nigeria to Daniel in Babylon; to Moses in Egypt, Elijah before Ahab, Peter and John before the counsel, and Paul before Jewish priests and Gentile rulers.

CHAPTER 2

THE ENSLAVEMENT OF IGBO NATION, AFTER INITIATION

THE CAUSE OF SLAVERY BY OGBONI CULT

- Hatred – Genesis 37:4-5

- Misrepresentation – Genesis 37:4

- Lack of vision and envy – Genesis 37:11

- Fear of a dreamer – Genesis 37:10,19

- Wickedness – Genesis 37:20, 23-24.

- Love of money – Genesis 37:26-28,36

- Famine and suffering – Genesis 41:1-3; 43:1-2; 46:5, 7

5 FACTS ABOUT IGBO'S HATRED IN THE PAST

— (GENESIS 37:4-5).

- They are hostile to themselves

- They suspect and hate each other without trust.

- They are proud and angry, or they feel injured when they see a fellow Igbo person who is better than them.

- They have anti-party spirit, hate unity, and work against it, but only among themselves.

- They detest leadership among themselves.

- They feel defeated and hate each other's progress.

5 FACTS ABOUT IGBO MISREPRESENTATION IN THE PAST

- They give false information against each other.

- They are unfair to each other.

- They mislead each other.

- They deceive each other.

- Their services are poor and improperly delivered when they represent their Igbo boss.

5 FACTS ABOUT IGBO ENVY AGAINST EACH OTHER

- They are uncomfortable at the progress of fellow Igbo

- Desire what others have and seek to destroy it.

- Wish others don't have what they have.

- Envy brings jealousy and unholy competition.

- Hate seeing other people's enjoyment or happiness.

5 FACTS ABOUT FEAR OF A DREAMER

- Igbo are dreamers, but they are afraid of anyone among them with greater dreams (Genesis 37:9-10, 19).

- They fight people with vision and excellencies.

- They fight to destroy people with goals in life, purpose for life, and with greater imagination.

- They fight people with great ideas or projects – a visionary.

- They fight creative people with greater experience.

5 FACTS ABOUT THE IGBO WICKEDNESS

(Genesis 37:20)

- A backslidden or fallen Igbo person is wicked against each other; they love strangers above their brothers.

- They are morally very bad against each other (Genesis 37:20, 23-24).

- They think evil, plan evil, and do evil against each other.

- They can cause harm, distress, or trouble against each other.

- They go beyond limit and reason in wickedness against each other.

5 FACTS RESULTS OF IGBO LOVE OF MONEY

(Genesis 37:26-28, 36)

- They are profit oriented and can prefer money above life once initiated (Genesis 37:26-28, 36).

- Their love for money leads them into all manner of crime.

- They can go to the extreme to get money.

- It leads them to desire temporal blessing above spiritual blessings (1Timothy 6:10; John 6:10-15, 25-35, 60, 66; Psalm 106:13-16).

- It leads them to seek for prosperity and abundance without holiness (Deuteronomy 32:5-6, 15; Jeremiah 22:21-22; Revelation 3.14-20).

6 STEPS THAT LED THE BACKSLIDDEN IGBO INTO FAMINE AND SUFFERING SUMMARIZED AGAIN

- Hatred against each other - Genesis 37:4-5

- Misrepresentation - Genesis 37:4

- Lack of vision, support, and envy - Genesis 37:11

- Fear of a dreamer - Genesis 37:9-10, 19

- Wickedness - Genesis 37:20, 23-24

- Love of money - Genesis 37:26-28, 36

REASONS FOR ENSLAVEMENT AND FAMINE

- (Genesis 41:1-3; 2 Kings 17:24, 29, 33, 41; Jeremiah 7:15-18; 44:15-18; Revelation 17:1-6, 15) (Famine of good people).

- Joseph was kidnapped and sold.

- Some Josephs died in sin, in prisons, and poisoned; others survived and ran to foreign lands.

CHAPTER 3

WHAT IS INTELLECTUAL CAPITAL?

(Daniel 6:1-5).

- The flight of intellectual capital is the migration of great people, writers, scientists, business moguls, and experts from Igbo land to other cities.

- It is taking away or the migration of intellectual materials that can be used to develop Igbo land to other cities.

- It is the migration of information, knowledge, wisdom, or talent from Igbo land to other cities.

- It is moving away or migration of markets, companies, industries, services, and technologies from Igbo land to other cities.

- It is employing Igbo brain for great ideas to develop industry, agriculture, business etc., for salary.

- It is the brain drain of Igbo talents for the development of other cities at the expense of Igbo land.

- Their intellectual capital converts money into products and gives employment to people in other cities.

- The migration of talented Igbo people contributes to the flight of money, job, and services that brought our people into joblessness, famine, crimes, and frustration.

- Wealth is based on knowledge, not on natural resources.

EFFECTS OF BIAFRA'S CIVIL WAR ON IGBO

- Blockages and denial of every good thing through evil policies in Nigeria against the Igbo before, during, and after the civil war (Joshua 6:1).

THE FLIGHT OF INTELLECTUAL IGBO

- The dreamer, a visionary moved to Egypt as a slave (Genesis 37:36).

- Joseph, an overseer, and a channel of blessings whisked out of Igbo land (Genesis 39.1-6, 21-23).

- Igbo, the spiritual scientists and nation developers, transferred to Egypt (Genesis 41:9, 14, 37-44, 57).

- Governors, leaders, and great Igbo with greatness and channel of blessings frustrated out of the land to foreign lands (Genesis 45:26, 28).

- The fruitful Igbo and God-fearing generals chased away (Exodus 1:7, 17, 19-21).

- Igbo, great deliverers and helpers, ran away to foreign lands (Exodus 2:16-19).

- Igbo, city builders and nation developers, rejected by their own people (Exodus 1:11, 13-14).

THE RESULTANT EFFECTS

- Digging the clay for making bricks – menial jobs.

- Kneading clay to proper consistency – profitless hard labor.

- Taking clay to brick molds – servants to their servants.

- Forming the bricks – working like Elephants and eating like rats.

- Drying them in the sun – working under sun and stress.

- Carrying them to building places – working over time without pay.

■ Building cities out of bricks – living under bondage and building without habitation (Deuteronomy 28:30-33, 38, 41).

■ After the war, the Igbo moved into all the cities of Nigeria, abandoned their land, went out as laborers, servants, and ordinary messengers to survive. They lost all their positions in all the offices in Nigeria, and their properties were declared as abandoned properties (Joshua 8:23, 27).

CHAPTER 4

PURPOSE OF LEADERSHIP

— (NUMBERS 27:16-21; ISAIAH 40:11; JOHN 10:2-4; 2 SAMUEL 5:2; 1SAIAH 55:4; HEBREWS 13:7, 17; 2 SAMUEL 23:3; 1 TIMOTHY 5:17; ACTS 20:28).

—

DEFINITION OF TRUE IGBO LEADERSHIP

- A leader is a minister, steward, and an elder who goes ahead of others and acts as guiding force.

- He is one who discovers the right thing to do; gives direction and structure to others.

- He is one who motivates and leads others toward a certain purpose, goal or course of action.

- He is one who holds the authority to lead with persuasion and example.

- A leader (shepherds of God's people) brings the sheep to green pasture of good spiritual and physical diet.

- He leads the sheep beside pure, clean, restful waters.

- Leaders guides the sheep in the right path to know what to do and enjoy God's perfect will in all things and at all times.

- True Igbo leader comforts the sheep with the rod of correction, not destruction.

- Leaders prepare satisfying diet to keep the sheep from wondering away from the flock.

- They anoint the head of each sheep with protective oil of the spirit to keep the flies and insects from bothering the sheep.

- True Igbo leaders are seen as captains, rulers, elders and as a result, must have eyes that can discern.

- Leaders must recognize the ability and potentials of the people they are assigned to lead.

- Leaders are supposed to focus on the positive area of the people they are elected to lead, not only on their negatives.

- True Igbo leaders challenge each person under their leadership to fulfil their potentials and gifts.

- True Igbo leaders are willing to spend time; labor and even get frustrated with each person without given up on them.

- They encourage each person in times of their weakness, mistakes and keep planting a bright vision in their heart.

- True Igbo leaders give people under them the opportunity to develop until they have confidence in what they are doing.

- The above and many are what the Igbo leaders in business, especially after the civil war demonstrated in business but our political leaders failed woefully, and unless they repent and do restitution they will pay for their wickedness, it's a promise.

The question is, why is Igbo land not developed? Why are we lacking such leaders to develop Igbo land?

CHAPTER 5

WHO ARE THE IGBO?

THE JOURNEY OF THE IGBO NATION

(Genesis 49:19; 12:1-3; 13:14-17).

- It is no longer hidden or a thing to be disputed that the Igbo are the children of Abraham, who entered into covenant with God.

- Igbo are the sons of Eri, the fifth son of Gad who left Egypt with his two younger brothers, namely: Arodi and Areli.

- Other of his relatives that joined them in the journey is Ijaw, Ido, Igala and Idoma, who made up the old eastern region in Nigeria - the South/ South and the South east.

- In their journey, they crossed over river Nile to Sudan (Old Ethiopia) to Chad, to Lokoja (present day Nigeria) via River Benue, and then through the River Niger.

- They eventually landed at Aguleri, around 1305 BC at the confluence of the two rivers, Ezu and Omambala (a tributary of the great river Niger).

- The evil spirits, demons, or fallen angels that settled in the land ages before their arrival confronted the Igbo ancestors and demanded for worship, but the great Eri refused (Isaiah 14:12; Jude 6).

- Eri moved into the hinterland to a place now known and called Enugu Aguleri and built a house, which as well served as an altar.

- He named the house 'Obi Gad' (Gad's house), in honor of his father, Gad, and dedicated the altar to God.

- Eri named his fourth son Heebo (Igbo) in commemoration of their origin (ref: *Aguleri: The Pivot*, pg 20).

- The word of identity, Igbo, came because of corruption of the Jewish word 'HEBREW'. The corruption evolved as follows: Hebrew-heebo-ebo/ibo (Igbo).

- According to the Encyclopedia Britanicca commentary on *Shinot* of 1929 and Torah commentary on *Shimot* of 1929 pointed to the Jewish origin of Ndi Igbo of South-eastern

Nigeria through a lineage of Gad, the seventh son of Jacob (Genesis 49:19).

- Eri was known to be very religious and resourceful. He was clever, intelligent, strong, courageous, and adventurous with leadership qualities.

- The worship of the only true God in Africa, except the North Africa of Egypt started first in Igbo land. Igbo ever before the coming of the missionaries in West Africa worshipped the God of Abraham, Isaac, and Jacob, their fathers.

- One of the biggest problems of Igbo nation is that they do not know their worth; so, they underrate, under value themselves and worship idol.

MORE EXPLAINATIONS

- Igbo names like Abraham's name is great. Through them, the nation, people that blesses them shall be blessed. Whoever curses them shall be cursed.

- God is the God of the Igbo and they shall possess the gates of their enemies (Genesis 12:1-3; 13:14-17; 15:1-27; 17:1-14; 22:15-18).

- Nigeria is blessed today because of the Igbo in their midst. Whatever problems Nigeria has today started when they started, maltreating, exploiting and killing the innocent Igbo in their midst.

- Igbo and true believers, ministers in Nigeria are the light and the salt of Nigeria. The day they were pushed out of their place in Nigeria, darkness took over Nigeria and life became bitter.

- However, the Igbo is the cause of their problems, not the Hausas or the Yoruba's. Why? How? They broke their covenant with God.

CHAPTER 6

GOD'S COVENANT WITH THE IGBO BROKEN

— (GENESIS 12:1-3; 49:19)

- As covenant children, God's purpose is to use the Igbo nation and African believers to introduce Himself; show the rest of the Nigerians and the world at large mercy and bless the entire Africa, but the Igbo failed.

- No nation would have had the power to keep the Igbo in bondage this long if they had remained with God.

- In times of war, Igbo are destined to fly over their enemies like the eagles (Exodus 19:3-4). To have victory over the enemies is the birth right of the Igbo.

- It is a common experience for an Igbo person to prosper beyond others anywhere in everything good.

- In the beginning, the most united people on earth were the Igbo, but today, the reverse is the case because of the foreign gods, cults in their midst. Why? They broke covenant with God and their unity was affected (Genesis 11:1, 6-8).

- In the beginning, the Igbo respected their leaders; listened to their elders and worked in unity but imported idols divided us to rule over us.

- In the beginning, the Igbo offered sacrifices to the true God, but today, their gods are multiplied.

- In the beginning, Igbo obeyed their leaders, but today, everyone goes their separate ways.

- In the past, they believed in one God, worshiped one God, and obeyed their elders. But today, even their elders have gone astray.

- In the beginning, the Igbo loved their language and spoke their language. But today, Igbo language is dying (Exodus 24:3-8; 34:27-28; Genesis 11:1-9).

- Igbo were covenant children with only one God. But today, they have broken that covenant, and entered into covenants with smaller gods.

- In the past, the Igbo were afraid of only one God. Today, they fear many gods.

- Igbo are problems to themselves, not any other people. God is not their problem; they are the one that left God, and God never left them.

- They fail to meet up with their own terms of covenant. God kept His, but Igbo failed.

CONDITION EACH IGBO PERSON MUST FULFILL

- God is looking; still searching for the Igbo to come back and keep His covenant (Exodus 19:5-6).

- God has fulfilled His promise before when the Igbo obeyed Him.

- He blessed them and made them number one in every state in Nigeria.

- They were specially blessed, identified everywhere in business, in politics, in education, and every good thing in Nigeria.

- They were God's servants in every office; known as priests and holy people who stood for the truth in every office until they backslid.

- They were known as preachers of God's word, God's righteousness, and teachers of the written word of God.

- The original Igbo did not contend against God's word. They obeyed every part of God's word to the letters, and compelled others to do so.

- They were covenant children, identified with one blood sacrifice (Exodus 24:7- 8; Revelation 12:11).

- On personal basis, Igbo individually were in covenant with God.

- They were in covenant with each other to obey God and His word.

- Their leaders were ready to spend time with God to pray until something happens.

- But today, every leader is selfish, spending time with false gods and evil spirits, and ignoring the only true God.

- God is searching for group of Igbo ministers, political leaders who He will hand over His program for the Igbo nation.

- He wants to work with covenant keepers; true covenant performers who will carry out His programs on earth from among the Igbo ministers.

- Igbo as kingdom of priests, an holy nation, and peculiar people are qualified for this position.

- As an Igbo person, you are qualified to answer the call. Respond, and God will empower you now (Deuteronomy 4:12-13).

- Igbo as priests in Nigeria to introduce the true worship of God, teach God's statues, and His true judgment are called.

- Igbo instead of taking their rightful position, compromised and yielded to false gods.

- Instead of keeping God's commandments, the Igbo bowed to the small gods; the idols of their coastal powers and the imported Ogboni power and Islamic cults.

- The first Igbo that joined Ogboni and other tribe's cult requested for money and they were given condition to be in charge of sacrifice, you will get details in the school.

- Igbo sold their strength to Ogboni cult from the west, to get money which God already gave them as their basic right being the covenant children of Abraham (Genesis 12:1-6; Romans 6:16).

- In the spiritual law, if you leave your God for another god, you become a slave to that god and the original owners of that god.

- Ogboni cult is elevated from ancestral coastal powers of the west to a cult beyond their region.

- As a result, Ogboni power is higher and more powerful than the ancestral coastal powers of the southeast because of willing submission. Why? Because Igbo refused to promote their coastal powers to a cult; which is right, but wrong and worse when they joined cult.

- The reason is because they pay allegiance, royalty, respect and honor to the only true God, the God of Abraham, Isaac and Jacob.

- When they backslid, they bowed to Ogboni cult, who is higher in rank than their coastal power that they refused to worship.

- Most unfortunately, the original owners, worshippers of Ogboni cult, were already being threatened by the prosperity of the Igbo.

- They were the only competitors of the Igbo in Nigeria in every area.

- Igbo who are very enterprising, industrious, and well known travellers were bewitched, manipulated, and they backslid (Deuteronomy 11:8, 9).

- They broke the commandment of God, and sold their strength and life span to Ogboni cult.

- The original owners of Ogboni cult initiated the first Igbo that joined Ogboni with unfavorable conditions.

- The secret on how to serve Ogboni was hidden from them.

- A careful study of Ogboni members in the west and east will prove this fact. We will discuss in Igbo class room in details.

- Igbo who are Ogboni members die young, have useless children, and lose their inheritance after a while.

- It happens to the owners of Ogboni cult, but not to the degree it happens to the Igbo members. Why? (2 Kings 17:26-28).

- The naked truth is that Igbo Ogboni members do not know the secret behind the worship of Ogboni cult and every other cult on earth.

- They do not know the terms of covenant; the details of the agreement; the secret behind Ogboni cult.

- That is why Igbo Ogboni cult members face early deaths of their business, destiny, children, wealth, and positions, and cannot rise up to certain level in Nigeria; in everything!

- The people who know the secret are not ready to reveal the truth and you cannot blame them because if the only rival you have, who is doing better than you exposes his secret, you will do better. You cannot blame them because no one wants to give his place to another.

- It is a place given to their tribe, and it will be foolish to just teach you how to rule over them. So, the fact is that as long as the Igbo refuse to come back to God, they will remain the slave tribe of Nigeria (1Samuel 7:3-4).

- And without God, no Pharaoh will willingly set her captive free. Ojukwu and others tried, but they did not have the spiritual power or commission from heaven. Therefore, what Ojukwu did not succeed to achieve with all the wealth of his father, no one can, except we turn back to our God. Thank God some Igbo ministers are now praying.

- Igbo are in unholy covenants, and unless they break it, they will remain slaves in the hands of the people they are destined to be better than.

- It is not the fault of the north and the west that we are slaves; it is our fault, because we are legal or lawful captives to the Ogboni and Islamic cult and other cults in the continent (Isaiah 49:24; Romans 6:16).

- Igbo were not forced to join Ogboni cult and other cults in the world; we did it willingly. Why am I saying we? Because we are a people, a nation of backslidden priests, who were represented by our backslidden ancestors (Joshua 9:15; 2 Samuel 21:1).

- A representative of any covenant is a legal representative, who stood for himself, children, and people forever (2 Samuel 21:1-2; 2 Kings 5:27).

- Our fathers made us servants by inheritance; they yielded and surrendered freely to Ogboni cult (Lamentation 5:7). Just like God does not have problem with David and the children of Israel, yet they suffered for famine for three years.

- As an Igbo believer or Christian, God may not have problem with you, yet you are in bondage, and all that you do does not prosper.

- There are people like that (2 Kings 4:1; Lamentation 5:1-22; James 4:7).

CHAPTER 7

THE WORST BACKSLIDING IN IGBO LAND

— DEUTERONOMY 18:9-14

- The worst backsliding in Igbo land is the backsliding of the church.

- The majority of the church in Nigeria has ceased from being the salt and the light of Nigeria.

- Many have retreated to their church buildings, preaching to themselves while evil prevail outside.

- Apart from few private schools, others are built by the missionaries.

- The church neglected schools and few unbelievers in the government took over the schools and destroyed the moral instructions.

- The occult people in Igbo land filled the government positions, every office, and the business.

- Believers neglected education and the Ogboni members took over.

- They are the ones found everywhere as leaders in every office, making things difficult for believers under them for serving God.

- They took over the court, business, and the law-making body; the management and the leadership.

- They believed that whoever controlled the educational system controlled the future agenda of the people.

- That is why so much pervasive evil is being openly portrayed in Igbo land for some time now. Edmund Burke said; "All that is necessary for evil to triumph is for good men to do nothing".

- It is wrong for believers to despise education and certain positions, like presidency, members of national and states assembly. We need good men who are in covenant with God to occupy every position.

- In some places today, to be rich, you have to join cults. Even to contest certain positions in government, you have to be rich and only few good people are rich because they do not belong to the cult.

THE WORST COMPROMISE

- So many Ogboni members, witches, and wizards, cultists have been empowered to enter the church.

- Many ministers of the gospel have been deceived to compromise their faith, and change their preaching to suit the occult people that sponsor their ministry.

- Instead of building lives, they build big cathedrals, filled with people who have no knowledge of God.

- The Igbo ministers envied these pastors and joined them in the evil competition, and God left many of them and their churches.

- Permit me to say that many gatherings in some churches today are the gatherings of witches and wizards (Psalm 74:7-9).

- The Igbo ministers, who are supposed to stand for the truth as the salt and light in Nigeria, joined the nation's backslidden pastors and God left them.

- Competition to be like other pastors in the land moved some Igbo pastors to compromise their faith.

THE INFLUENCE OF THE SOCIETY

- What the Igbo have is what the nation needs to make progress anywhere in the world.

- Igbo as covenant people of God are a channel God wants to use to takeover Nigeria but they allowed the devil to deceive them.

- Igbo ministers made the matter worst by compromising with the nation's backsliding churches to influence them negatively (Hosea 7:8, 9). They mixed themselves with strangers and lost their relationship with God.

- They wanted to be like others, so they put God aside and compromised their faith (1Samuel 8:19, 20).

COVETOUSNESS AND COMPROMISE

- So many churches with fine buildings, nice messages, and well packaged deliverance materials have no God in them.

- They have money, machines, and notable programs, but they lack born again ministers.

- They have followers, sponsors, and every good thing on earth, but they are not in good relationship with God.

- Their pastors are witches and wizards, trouble makers, and money-making charismatic machine guns.

- They are in cults, though they preach well, but they lack godly character (Genesis 13:10, 12-13).

- The lives of their ministers are blessed with every good thing physically but they are wicked and devilish.

- Their fake prosperities influenced Igbo ministers and they joined them.

- That was how Igbo ministers sold their birth right.

LUST OF THE FLESH

- It is no longer hidden to believe that many ministers are not called by God.

- Many churches are established by people in the cults. They take titles, answer apostles, prophets, etc., but they are false.

- Even Satan establishes church these days and prospers the pastors he ordained.

- It is called deliverance, counterfeits of Satan. Let the Bible speak (Exodus 7:10-13, 20-22; 8:5-7, 20-23; 1Samuel 18:10, 11; Ezekiel 9:1-4; Revelation 13:11-17; 2 Thessalonians 2:7-12).

- In the old days, if a Christian commits immorality, the result is destructive. Some die in the very act. But today, the more fake miracle they perform, the more they do evil, the more they prosper.

- The more they break God's commandment and do wicked things, the more they prosper.

- That is to prove to you that they are not working for God (Mathew 7:21-23; Psalm 74:1-11).

- The true Igbo ministers saw it, lusted after it, practiced, and lost their ministry.

- Others died and their great ministries scattered.

- God may not allow you to continue your work if you commit certain sins and refuse to repent and come back to faith. They need deliverance together with their members.

- People who receive anointing to start a church from the occult world can live anyhow, but not all the ones that are called by God will do so and live anyhow, especially Igbo ministers, check.

- Why are Igbo churches not growing, you may be asking? Igbo are covenant children of God, and must keep the covenant to prosper.

- They are not ordinary people or just someone. They are kingdom of priests.

- Some of them, the Igbo in unconscious manipulation or under attacks, who seems to be prospering, need to close down their ministry and seek for God's deliverance outside their ministry.

- When you see a prosperous minister or ministry who is greedy, proud, immoral, jealous, and covetous and with anger, yet his ministry prospers, he is working for the devil.

- A minister who is really called by God and along the line backslide and is ready to work for the devil, can be allowed by the devil to prosper, gather crowd, and perform fake miracles (Matthew 7:21-23; Revelation 13:11-17).

- If you are not ready to work with the devil and yet you commit sin, you either lose your life or your ministry.

- Many Igbo ministers want to have their cake and eat it (Jeremiah 44:15-18).

- Many Ogboni members today pastor big churches and prosper greatly.

- It takes the grace of God to understand some level of satanic deceit (2 Corinthians 11:13-15).

- When sin enters and takes over a person (a minister called by God) and he accepts it as a lifestyle, the devil will take over him and run his ministry for him with fake miracles and those miracles will be unprofitable.

- With time, the deceived minister will get used to it and the followers will accept it.

- A pastor or ministry that condones the love of money, pride, self-indulgence, and prayerlessness with multiple activities to make money is an agent of the devil, no matter the good things he do.

CHAPTER 8

THE COMPROMISE OF IGBO MINISTERS

CASES OF COMPROMISE

- **AARON** was called of God, but he yielded to the pressures around him and compromised in the area of false worship (Exodus 32:21-24).

- **JACOB** compromised and under his mother's influence, he yielded on moral standard to win his brother, Esau, in a battle to gain material things, achieve greatness, and reach a manmade goal (Genesis 27:6-19).

- Others compromise because of the crave for popularity and praise while some on the area of women, unhealthy relationship with people with different conviction, unsuitable doctrines, associating with people with low morals and principles. Compromise can lead a person to modify the truth and his lifestyle to conform to the world (1 Kings 11:1-8; Nehemiah 13:26; 2 Chronicles 18:1-7; 19:1; Acts 21:18-36).

- Love and cares of this world (2 Timothy 4:10; Mark 16:18).

- Self-indulgence (Genesis 9:1, 20-21).

- Love of money (1Timothy 6:9, 10; John 13:29; Joshua 7:20-21).

- Unbelief and prayerlessness (Hebrews 3:12; Psalm 78:18-22; 2 Kings 1:2-4; Mathew 26:40, 41, 58).

- Using God to make money with multiplied activities (Song of Solomon 1:6; 2 Chronicles 25:14-16).

PUNISHMENT FOR BACKSLIDDEN IGBO

- God sees backslidden Igbo as traitors, outcasts, captives, and people with leprosy.

- The day Igbo ministers backslid, everything worked against them.

- It is wrong for the Igbo to see any other tribe as their major problem, idolatry is because no Igbo person should join others to worship idol, we are different and God's seed.

- Anyone who attacks the Igbo will suffer, but the Igbo are the cause. The reason is because they broke God's covenant with them.

- When the Igbo traders joined Ogboni cult, God endured it. When their traditional rulers and politicians did the same, God was still with the Igbo. But when the minister's backslid, God cast them out and all Igbo race were affected.

- Their prayers became abominable before God (Jeremiah 7:15-18).

- When God forsook the Igbo, Satan attacked them; satanic agents prevailed over them.

- Our names as a nation was removed from the book of life, and the wrath of God came on us (Exodus 32:33; Ezra 8:22).

If you enter into covenant with God and turn around to break it, God's wrath will come upon you (Job 34:26, 27).

■ Igbo were rejected, cast out by God. They became dead spiritually, and was exposed to satanic attacks.

■ If we are talking about marginalization, slavery, or being neglected in Nigeria, Satan enslaved us before he handed us over to our brethren in Nigeria (1Timothy 5:15).

■ We are the ones who sold ourselves over to Satan and his agents in Nigeria.

■ Our backsliding exposed us to demonic attacks, sickness, terrors, shame, punishments, and sorrows. If we repent today, everything will change.

■ Many Igbo people may disagree with me, attack me and decide not to repent but the few that will repent can change the whole curse to blessings.

WHAT BACKSLIDING CAUSED THE IGBO

Absence Of Leadership: Genesis 11:1-9.

- Have you asked yourself how the saying that Igbo have no leader came about? In the beginning, Igbo were the most united tribe in Nigeria.

- Their disunity started after they backslid and turned their back from God.

- Igbo are facing attacks from the coastal powers of Igbo land, the imported Ogboni cult, other foreign gods, and rejection from God.

- In the spiritual ranking, Ogboni having been accepted and elevated into cult is higher than the demoted coastal powers of Igbo land (Romans 6:16).

- Ogboni came to Igbo land and subdued the resident coastal powers and scattered the Igbo, put them into enmity, and divided them so as to have rule over them.

- When a carnal leader backslides, the spiritual leader will restore him. But if a spiritual leader backslides, there will be confusion.

■ That is the problem with Igbo nation. Both leaders have backslidden and none can help each other (Exodus 32:1; Judges 17:6).

■ Until Igbo ministers humble themselves, forget their differences, break denominational barrier, put aside their pride and ego, repent, and seek God's face, Igbo tribe will remain slaves in Nigeria.

■ Our problem is that both Moses and Aaron in Igbo land have backslidden; mixed themselves among ordinary people and the worst is that we did not know (Hosea 4:6).

■ Igbo ministers who are blaming their politicians are blinded because they are worse.

■ If Igbo ministers do not have a recognized leader, a voice among them, how can the carnal leaders, the politicians have?

LEADERSHIP BAD EXAMPLES

- Lack of unity brings carelessness, independent evil lifestyles, and license to sin.

- When you see your spiritual leader living in sin, the ignorant ones will copy the evil lifestyle.

- If you know that you are expected to give account, you will be careful.

- If the spiritual leaders are careless, the political leaders, head of government will be careless (Isaiah 56:10-12).

- Igbo do not support each other; they are independent and ready to support people from other tribes rather than themselves. It is a curse and only God can deliver us.

IMMORALITY AND LOVE OF MONEY

- I have watched ministers' life from other tribes and Igbo tribe alike.

- Both had the same problem: They love money and immorality.

- Both fall victim, but an Igbo person lost his ministry while the other did not.

- From my finding, Igbo are naturally covenant children.

- Their covenants are different, so it made me to be a little careful.

- I studied the lives of the Levites in Israel and ordinary Israelites and discovered that God is angrier with the Levites when they break the law than ordinary Israelites.

- When I hear people from other tribes say that Igbo love money, I understand them very well.

- What they are saying is that we love money more than you but you are a different people. You are a covenant child and you are not expected to love money the way we do.

- A real priest of God, an Igbo minister, called of God, cannot indulge in immorality and retain his life or ministry, unless he is an occultist (Leviticus 10:1-2).

- Igbo ministers must not compete with other ministers in unrighteousness.

- You may point one or two Igbo ministers who live in sin, yet they are alive. True, but how much life do they have. What is the number of their congregation and total branches?

- Igbo anywhere, whether in the government or ministry are not meant to serve idols, do evil, or practice iniquity (1Samuel 2:12-17, 22; 8:10-21; Jeremiah 23:9-16).

- There are things that I know that if I do, I may not wake up the next day, and if I wake up, my conscience will almost kill me. But I see others do them and walk in the street as if nothing happened.

- They still preach, sing, and conduct deliverance more than me with lies. I do not envy them because I have a different covenant (Mathew 7:21-23).

FALSE PROPHECY, DECEIT, AND FAKE ANOINTING

- To be frank, in our neighboring tribes, there are genuine, true and great ministers with life-saving, pure miracles from God through the operation of the gifts of the Holy Spirit in their lives and ministries.

- This is the reason why this nation is still experiencing greatness and has not died spiritually and physically.

- They are truly, wholly, and consistently men of God to be emulated.

- We do not have many of their likes in Igbo land, not even the whole Africa.

- However, their tribe's men under them are extremely bad, occultists, and tribally demonized and money mongers.

- My fears are that by the time these men expire (because one day, they will), they may not have a replacement.

- They are fine gentlemen, surrounded by lieutenants of tribe's men with bad characters.

- Tribes backslidden ministers, filled with all manner of lusts, worldliness, love of money and ready to kill whoever oppose them, including respected God's anointed leaders of their own tribes.

- I wish I am wrong, but I am not. They may die with their revival spirit and darkness will capture this nation.

- Our nation is filled with many mighty church buildings with ministers who are possessed with the spirit of false prophecies, desire for temporal blessings above spiritual things, desires for abundance and evil prosperity. The nation is filled with ministers with partial obedience - unfaithfulness without righteousness.

- This is a call for Igbo ministers to come back to God and seek Him afresh for renewed anointing and the power of the Holy Ghost.

CHAPTER 9

IGBO LEADERS AND THEIR CHARACTERS

WRONG ASSUMPTION OF LEADERSHIP POSITION

- It is dangerous, disastrous, self-centered, un-anointed or uninspired leaders who assume leadership privilege by favor, pride or by force (Acts 5:33-38).

- Having proved that Igbo problems are spiritually linked, the qualification of their leaders must not only be based on physical fitness, academic qualifications, professional experience, social qualities, and success management principles.

- It must be a combination of the above. Secular knowledge must not be exalted above scriptural knowledge. We must not allow worldly wisdom to take the place of divine wisdom. There must be a balance.

- Biblical and human history both give enough evidence that no group or nation can rise above the level of the quality of its leadership (Zechariah 13:7; Mathew 9:36; Numbers 27:16-17; Judges 2:7, 10-11).

- If the leader is strong, the people under him will be strong. The defeat of the leader is the defeat of the led.

- A leader that has no vision will not influence people under him to make progress.

- The biggest problem of the Igbo nation is leadership, spiritual and physical.

- Our leaders are selfish and do not plan for Igbo as a people.

- The Igbo are like sheep without shepherds.

- My fear is that if in this generation, our present leaders fail to plan and develop our region, and it will be disastrous.

- We need leaders that will gather the Igbo in Igbo land, settle the Igbo in Igbo land, and establish the Igbo in Igbo land.

- The Igbo are scattered in Nigeria like sheep that has no shepherd.

- We need programs, policies, and business centre that will bring the Igbo back to the land.

- If we are agitating for Biafra without planning; it is foolishness.

- Vatican City is a nation in another nation, not under a nation; it is policies in place that matters.

- Shouting for Igbo liberation, Biafra, or another nation is good but without planning, is useless and lack of foresight.

- Our leaders should plan to bring all our people back; not out of Nigeria for now, but out of slavery and effortlessly if its God will it will happen without struggle.

- The spiritual leaders, pastors, reverends, bishops, or every denomination must be involved.

How do we do that?

- Firstly, all leaders should examine themselves, make peace with God and thereafter, bring the congregation under them back to God.

- This is called congregational deliverance.

- When I listen to Igbo youths in social media, I become ashamed and afraid.

- Our youths do not know our history and our relationship with God.

- Igbo land is deserted at the mercy of other cities in Nigeria.

- It is like an abandoned land, full of failures. Only the governors, workers under them, and few business men are reasonably useful.

- Igbo land is virtually populated by people who failed in business and jobs outside Igbo land, jobless youths and elders who settle down into kidnapping and cause trouble in the land.

- It is the responsibility of our governors, senators, and every leader in Igbo land to give these jobless youths jobs.

HOW CAN WE ACHIEVE THIS?

- Very simply, Igbo have developed other cities in Nigeria, so let us develop ours.

- The Ohaneze should come out with one decision and write our needs down as a people to the federal government.

- If they want our vote in the next election and every election, they should help us develop our land.

- This is not the time to collect money and share. We need to think of our land.

- Let them build our city, tar our roads, build our bridges, dredge River Niger, and bring sea port to the east.

- Let the five governors, irrespective of their party come together, plan together and bring back security in Igbo land.

- Let them give us land for industrialization of the Igbo land.

- Let them compel our business men, our national assembly members, old and new politicians to bring their money and invest it in our land.

- Let us build factories and companies that will give jobs to our youths.

- We can do it; it is possible if we can have an agreement.

- Our Christian fathers must unite, preach the sound truth, and move our people to serve God (Judges 2:7, 10-11).

- We want to pray together again, have a common front, bring God back to our land, and ask for God's empowerment - gifts of the Holy Ghost.

- When our Christian leaders are empowered, people from all over the world will come to seek for our God in Igbo land.

- If we pray, God will raise mighty men and women of God in Igbo land.

- Our prayers should be; "O Lord, raise men and women after God's heart; truly empowered ministers."

- Men of righteousness, who are preferred above others; with excellent spirit, sent by God, chosen vessels, and recognized worldwide; strong ministers whose hearts are towards God, not towards money, sex, or worldliness.

- Renewed and anointed ministers; mature men and women of God.

- We need ministers of God in Igbo land who are saved, zealous, self-denying and self-emptying.

- Ministers of God, who are clothed with humility; wise as serpent and harmless as doves.

- Simple as children, compassionate as the Savior, strong in faith, and not staggering at the promise of God.

- We need ministers who are approved unto God, a workman that needed not to be ashamed, rightly dividing the scriptures.

- We need ministers in Igbo land who can lock and unlock, bind and loose, and who are crucified to the world and the world is crucified in them.

- We need ministers of God who are energized by the spirit, and in who the rivers of living water flow unhindered out of their belly.

- We need true ministers of God in Igbo land who are truly the temple of God, with the fruit and gifts of the Spirit in evidence. This should be our focus as ministers in Igbo land and that is what we must get.

- We need ministers and members who will be used to bring revival in Igbo land.

- Ministers who will be yielded in God's hand as the clay in the potter's hand; purged, inflamed, sanctified, anointed, and empowered.

- Igbo land is tired of occult pastors; lazy, selfish, careless, indifferent, worldly, money-loving, magical, and carnal demonstrating ministers.

- When we get this set of ministers, there will be revival in Igbo land and light will come (Judges 2:7, 10-11).

- We do not want to leave a generation that does not know God behind.

- We want to produce leaders with godly character, and it has to start with the ministers.

- Only God through our prayers can raise leaders of godly character, divine ability, and spiritual wisdom to lead the Igbo out of slavery.

- Without strong leadership, the Igbo nation will remain behind in everything.

- It will take courageous and godly leaders to rise up against idolatry, sin, and witchcraft practices.

- Igbo are lacking God-given leaders, and that is why we cannot confront the powers in the land (Judges 2:18-19).

- It is our prayer that will bring leaders that will bring justice and deliverance from poverty, joblessness, and all manner of problems. I am not a Muslim, but I like the way they hold fast their faith in their religion. Though in Nigeria, they fought and established sharia court.

- Igbo needs to practice Christianity which is our inheritance.

- We need kings in Igbo land; traditional leaders who will practice traditional Christianity, not idolatry or ogbonalization of our communities.

- We need kings in every community who will support God's work, sponsor God's work, promote God's work, and lead the community to Christ (Judges 2:25).

THE YOUTHS ARE TIRED

- From my observation, the youth in Igbo land want change and they are readily waiting for divine leadership.

- They want to do away with Ogboni cult, idolatry, fetishism, witchcraft, occultism, animism, traditional religion, inclination to evil customs, and superstitious beliefs that contradict Christ (Colossians 2:8).

- They want to serve the only true God, the God of Abraham, Isaac, and Jacob.

- They want to work under traditional leaders with traditional Christian beliefs; born again Igwes and royal highnesses.

- Leaders who are occultist, idolatrous, childish, and babyish are our problems.

- Unborn-again leaders are the cause of our oppression, God's judgment, slavery, and every problem.

Let the scriptures speak:

> "For, behold, the Lord, the LORD of hosts, doth take away from Jerusalem and from Judah the stay and the staff, the whole stay of bread, and the whole stay of water, The mighty man, and the man of war, the judge, and the prophet, and the prudent, and the ancient, The captain of fifty, and the honorable man, and the counsellor, and the cunning artificer, and the eloquent orator.

And I will give children to be their princes, and babes shall rule over them. And the people shall be oppressed, everyone by another, and every one by his neighbor: the child shall behave himself proudly against the ancient, and the base against the honorable." (Isaiah 3:1-5)

CHAPTER 10

CHANGE OF CHARACTER

COMMITMENT FOR CHANGE

- God expects commitment to Him, His Word, and to the people at all cost, before true change will come.

- Commitment for the people (John 10:11-12).

- Commitment like soldiers in the army (2 Timothy 2:3, 4).

- Commitment to obey God's word at all cost (Jude 3; Revelation 22:18, 19).

WHAT IS CHARACTER?

- Character is the sum of all the qualities in a person's life, exemplified by one's thoughts, habit, values, motives, attitudes, feelings, and actions.

- Character is not only how a person acts, it includes the inner thoughts, motives, and attitudes producing the actions.

- Character is not what a person thinks, says, and does when he is not under pressure and temptation.

- True character is revealed by what you are when temptation, pressure, and affliction come.

- Character is not only that behavior or conduct which other people see on the external; it is also that which people do not see, but known to God and you alone.

- Character is not only how you relate and treat people in the public; it includes how you treat people or behave where nobody sees you or knows what you do.

- Character is what you are before God, before your conscience, and before all people at all times in every situation and condition in life.

HOW DO WE KNOW A GOOD LEADER?

- A good leader must be of a noble character before God and before all men.

- Character in your spiritual life, personal life and academic life must honor God.

- A good leader must have integrity, be faithful, and committed to the people he leads.

- He must have the right motive and attitude.

- He must have a shepherd heart, stability, and ability to get along with others.

- He must be a lover of people, be gracious, with submissive mind and listening ears.

- He must be humble, respectful, and good in communication.

- He must be transparent, open, and honest.

- A leader's friend, where he goes and what he does reflect the kind of person he is.

HOW TO DICTATE BAD LEADERS?

- Bad leaders do not think, plan, or accept the responsibilities of developing their land.

- Their investments are outside Igbo land or their place of origin.

- They think and plan only about their security and for their family without planning for the security of people under them.

- They do not fight against anti-security agents because they are protected with them.

- They do not plan or fight for the lasting security of the jobless youth; they use and dump them.

- They are occultists, wicked, and they make money with people's destiny (Acts 16:16, 19).

CHAPTER 11

OPPOSITION TO DEVELOPMENT

— ACTS 4:13-21

- There are people in Igbo land who are deeply committed to idolatry, occultism, animism, demonic traditional religion, and evil customs and superstitious beliefs.

- These groups of people hate development, change, and God's presence in every city. Others are possessed by the spirit of denomination and hatred to unity.

- They are unborn-again church elders, who hate the spread of good things; deliverance of people they bound with problems spiritually.

- They hate community liberation from collective captivity (Acts 4:14-22; 15:17, 18, 25-28).

- The call to return to God is upon all the Igbo because only God can bring the desired unity in Igbo land.

- With unity from God, irrespective of our party, denomination, or background, our land will be developed.

- Our generation is a chosen generation to bring back true worship that will sustain development in our land.

- This time, we do not want to see anyone who will raise opposition to this movement to develop Igbo land (Acts 6:11-15).

- We want all our traditional rulers, elders of every community in Igbo land, and good people of the land to sponsor prayer team in every community so that each community leader will hand his community to God afresh for prayers.

- Let no community leader block the way or oppose the spiritual development. True development takes place in the spirit before it will manifest physically.

- We do not want any occultist or evil leader to stir up the youth for violence.

- The development we are talking about will provide jobs for our youths; end the business of kidnapping, armed robbery, and assassination business.

- We beg all traditional and evil gang leaders in Igbo land benefiting from such business to stop and allow our youths to come to God who will change their lives, better their future, and the future of our born and unborn children.

- We want to invite God, hand our community to Him, and end violence in Igbo land.

- Let all our elders, the learned, and every class co-operate. We are not going to destroy or fight our customs or a tradition that promotes prosperity (Colossians 2:8).

- Some of this evil custom, traditions have destroyed Igbo land.

- Ogboni cult is the brain behind the migration of great destined Igbo to the other land.

- Paul was a traditionalist, an arch defender of his inherited customs and leader of local and international rulers.

- He was a religious fanatic; he profited so much in his father's religion above all his equals in his own nation.

- He was an observer of traditions, more zealous than all and even killed and sacrificed human beings, but the result was that he ended up scattering his nation. Good people left the city. All that were destined for greatness to develop the nation ran away.

- Paul was not just an assassinator; he has an organization that does the job for him. He had permission, license, and written authority to kidnap whoever he wished (Galatians 1:13-14).

- The major result was that he scattered good people and his nation was abandoned undeveloped (Acts 8:1-3).

- He put people to death, stoned Stephen, a man filled with the Holy Ghost, full of faith, power, great wonders and miracles.

- Paul stirred up people, elders, and scribes under his occult activities in his nation; scattered people who were destined to develop the land, and they travelled abroad and used their talent to develop other cities.

- Paul caused havoc and entered into every house in the land for destruction.

- Paul was known as a kidnapper; a killer, who hailed men and women, committed them to prison without being challenged. If you are like Paul in your community, please repent because the youths are tired of joblessness.

- Release them from your altars and allow them to serve God. Come out as a community leader to hand over your community, people and the land to Christ, we beg you.

- Herod was a king like many of our traditional kings who hate development. He killed James, the brother of John with the sword.

- Maybe you are the one in charge of killing the business of young men in your community or you are responsible for young ladies not getting married, barrenness, profitless hard labor and wasted efforts of the people of your communities.

- It is possible that you have used your Ogboni power to bewitch every destiny in your community. I will advise you, repent, support spiritual development in your community and hand over your community to Christ for liberation.

- Remember, Herod was beyond human destruction (Acts 12:1-3). He was so anxious for power from the occult world. He was empowered until evil power overpowered him and used him at will.

- He bewitched people and influenced them to accept his wickedness.

- He arrested Peter, the head of the spiritual developers, and locked him up. But God raised a vibrant prayer team; divine militant soldiers, who prayed and Peter was released without negotiation.

- When God wanted to judge Herod, He did not use cancer, earthquake, atomic bomb, Ebola, Coronavirus or angel of death. He used the weakest creature that feed with his flesh and drank his blood while he still lived, until he gave up the ghost.

- You may be an undefiled witch or wizard, a sorcerer or a false prophet, hindering God's people and destroying the destinies of the youth.

- There was a person like that in a place called Paphos (Acts 13:6-8). He was a Jew and his surname Bar-Jesus. He manipulated himself into the people in the government and made sure they do not develop the city.

- He controlled the deputy of that country called Sergius Paulus, a prudent man who was ready to develop the city.

- You may be the one collecting the government money meant to develop your community, suffering the youth and keeping them jobless. This time, if you try it, God forbid, you will be blinded, exposed to all manner of shame, disgrace, reproach, failures and defeats.

- You may be in covenant with Ogboni cult or traditional demons, and as a result, you sold your community to the devil and they are wholly given to idolatry (Acts 17:6). It has happened before in other cities.

- Idolatry may be the source of your business, your trade or means of livelihood. You need to repent and ask Christ to redirect you.

- Demetrius was a silversmith, which made silver shrines for a god called Diana. He was very wealthy and a whole continent and people all over the world came to buy small gods from him. Yours is just a local cult; a small god.

- Diana was first class world recognized cult; yet, the spiritual developers destroyed it and overthrow their priests (Acts 19:24-27).

- Your community must be handed over to Christ because the youths are tired of suffering; tired of bewitchments, untimely deaths, business failures, useless lives, and marital failures.

- They want development and that is what we are begging our traditional rulers to help us achieve.

- Allow the youth to enter the community with the gospel, prayers of liberation, and solemn assemble.

HOW DO WE DEAL WITH OPPOSITION?

- When Paul arrived Athens with spiritual developmental message, he met a great challenge.

- The city was sophisticated and idolatrous.

- The structures and buildings were massive and impressive like the building of our rich Igbo without industries to develop lives.

- It was the home of many of the scholars and orators of that age.

- They had education, architectures, pleasures, social development, and other physical materials.

- Though with this physical development, the city was spiritually empty.

- The people were wholly given to idolatry, superstition, vain philosophy, pleasures, idle curiosity, spiritual blindness, materialism, and sinful lifestyles (Acts 17:16-31; 19:28, 29).

HOW DID PAUL PREACH?

- He did not use physical tools or instruments to destroy the idols in the city.

- He confronted their ignorance with the everlasting truth; their darkness with eternal light, and confronted sinners with eternal life.

- At the end, some mocked, others delayed their day of salvation. Yet among the high and the lowly, some believed unto eternal life (Acts 17:16-34).

- Therefore, we are not going to use force or physical weapon to start this great work.

- One thing we have to bear in mind is that every community and all that live in it is created by God, including the traditional rulers.

- Therefore, it is an honor for the traditional rulers and the elders to be asked to hand the land to God.

- If he refuses, another person can do that but that traditional ruler will be reported to God (Jeremiah 32:17). There is nothing too hard for God to do.

- The entire spiritual leaders in every community must pray and fast to tell God what they want in their communities (Mathew 17:20-21; 21:21-22).

- If they have faith and believe in their God, no power can stop them. Their prayers will be answered.

- Any evil person in that community that blocked spiritual development, crusade, and community liberation will be removed.

- Believers in any community have the final say, not the unrepentant occult men or women. No witch or wizard will stand against true prayer team in any community.

- If we pray and take over every community and every state in Igbo land spiritually, bring down spiritual light and spiritual development, no occult power can stop us.

- Believers have the key for the development of Igbo land. We have suffered enough in the hand of the people that we are better than.

- Our born and unborn children and God will not congratulate us for developing the north, south and west without developing our own place.

- It is a shame and an outstanding rebuke to be a servant to our servants (Zechariah 4:5-7; Hebrews 13:8; John 8:28; Philippians 2:5-9).

- I challenge anyone from Igbo land to show me any part of Nigerian constitution or law of any nation that is against the development of Igbo nation. If none; then I have not offended anyone.

HOW THEN ARE WE GOING TO START?

- Satan, evil spirits, coastal powers of Igbo land, and imported evil forces are behind the underdeveloped Igbo land.

- We must pull down their entire stronghold and dislodge every demon in the territory of Igbo land.

- Every Igbo person must be involved in this spiritual warfare, irrespective of their denomination.

- The only qualification is to be an Igbo born, a lover of the Igbo, and the third is for you to give your life to Christ, which is most important.

- We must have the determination to succeed (John 4:34; 9:4; Acts 20:20-24; 21:13, 14; Mathew 10:16, 17; Proverbs 4:7; 9:1; Philippians 4:13).

- There must be readiness to follow through in spite of any opposition; even if I die, let others continue. We need freedom, not a country because we are a country already, until God decides otherwise.

- There shall be no pettiness and self-pity. We must not yield or surrender to discouragement.

CHAPTER 12

OBEDIENCE; GOD'S DEMAND

- As a covenant people of God, the Igbo have only one step against the development of their land, and that is disobedience to God.

- As for God, He is faithful to keep His own part if only we can obey.

- For example, the land He promised to give the children of Israel was in the hands of Israel's enemies at that time.

- When they left Egypt, all the original owners of the land were determined never to allow them into the land.

- Other things like the Red Sea, evil forests, and the wild animals living in them at that time showed that it was impossible to get there.

- All the great nations on the way were a big threat. The oppositions were too much, including the wall of Jericho.

- The Amorites, Jebusites, Havites, Canaanites, and numerous '…ites' were a big threat, but God re-assured them again that it was possible (Deuteronomy 30:1-10).

- Despite all these enemies, the children of Israel conquered all the enemies, entered the land, and possessed it (Joshua 21:43-45).

- The Lord fulfilled His own part of the covenant, gave them all the land, caused them to possess it, and they are presently living in that land.

- Despite all their enemies' gang ups until now, the children of Israel, our own blood, developed their land.

- Israel is the most developed land in the whole Middle East and the strongest military wise.

- All over the world, wherever they are, they are the developers and with this evidence, why can't we develop our own land? "DISOBEDIENT" (Exodus 19:5-6; Deuteronomy 11:8-9).

- The only thing standing between us and the development of Igbo land is disobedience and if only we can obey His voice and keep His commandments, the matter will be settled.

- As for the personal resources and everything we need to develop Igbo land, they are available; the only thing we lack is obedience.

- If we can keep God's commandment, the strength will be released.

- Igbo land if cleansed and delivered is a land that is fertile for prosperity of all kind.

- It is a land where God promised to promote people above others.

- It is a land that is possessed with all manner of blessings.

- It is a land that every factory and industry that is established there will grow and overtake others.

- It is a place of increase, multiplications, and storage.

- It is a land that brings good things in and supplies good things out to the entire world.

- It is a land that enemies that attack it will be smitten or subdued.

- It is a land of preservation, full of store houses.

- It is a land of prosperity that can grow small businesses to multinationals.

- It is a land of settlement, establishment, and holiness.

- It is a land where ministries and ministers prosper greatly.

- It is a land of plenty of good things, fruitfulness, and good treasures.

- It is a land that people can easily come and connect with God to receive deliverance, healing, and salvation.

- It is a land where rain from heaven drops to bless the works done in it.

- It is a land of science and scientific discoveries.

- Igbo land is where many nations must come and borrow from.

- It is a land where anything that is done in it will rise above others as the head.

- It is a land that is destined to stay on top of other lands in the land. But reverse is the case because of disobedience (Deuteronomy 28:1-14; Joshua 1:5-8).

- Igbo who move out to other cities and develop them are just the carriers of little blessings from the land.

- The main blessings are in the land, hidden by disobedience and can easily be discovered by obedience.

- If the Igbo obey the Lord, repent of their sins, forsake idolatry, and develop their land, no man will be able to stand against them in any area of life.

- If the governors, national/state assembly members, the businessmen in and outside Igbo land use the little resources with them, the above can be achieves in few years.

- The way God helped the American Jews, Russian Jews, British Jews, and the Jews in their land today, He will be with the Igbo.

- He promised not to fail us nor forsake us if we obey. What we need now is just courage and obedience, and the miracle will take place.

- Igbo land will be flooded with heavenly blessings. It will be like a dream when we start.

- God wants the Igbo to serve Him with perfect heart, especially our ministers.

- If we approach Him with willing minds, seek and keep His commandments, He will develop our land and prosper us above others (2 Chronicles 28:9, 10).

- Our continued rebellion and refusal to serve only God is the reason why we are suffering, not our brethren from other tribes.

- If we put away evil, do the right thing, learn and do well, God will empower us to develop our land without helps from the federal government.

- If we reject idolatry and occultism and seek judgment, relieve the oppressed, and help the helpless among us, God will cause us to enjoy the good things in this nation.

- If we obey the Lord, serve Him, fear Him, and offer sacrifice half the way we have done to Ogboni gods and coastal powers, Igbo tribe will be great.

- Let the scriptures speak (2 Chronicles 15:1, 2; Isaiah 1:16-20; 1 Samuel 15:22; 1 Peter 1:14-16; 4:17-19; Hebrews 5:8, 9).

- Let me make it clear; no liberator can liberate the Igbo outside us. Do not be deceived, running up and down for deliverance from ministers from other tribes.

- We can do it ourselves by simple obedience through true repentance.

- No one can get God's support without obeying His word in continuous obedience (Acts 5:33-38).

- Repentance and obedience to God's word is the only way for the Igbo' liberation.

- Even if the federal government of Nigeria gives us one thousand Biafra's, Igbo can never be free without true repentance. I stand to be corrected!

- You can fight for Biafra, trouble the federal government, and get the support of America and the United Nations, which is good, but our problem can never be solved without a good relationship with God.

- By the way, what is the meaning of Biafra? Find out yourself, it's a great name with powerful meaning.

- Many people who are agitating for Biafra are seeking the attention of Aso Rock to collect money and enrich their personal pockets, except few.

- They are like Theudas, boasting to be somebody to deceive the Igbo.

- Many of those who ignorantly follow them to shout Biafra end up in prison, and others die without burial. Is that what we want? It is foolishness to follow Judas because followers of Judas never survived; they perish (Acts 5:37).

- The question is; what do we need from Nigeria, Abuja, Aso Rock and every Nigerian? I can answer.

CHAPTER 13

WHAT THE IGBO NEED FROM NIGERIA

— (2 CHRONICLES 36:22-23; EZRA 1:1-4,
7-11; NEHEMIAH 2:1-9).

- Having said all, the truth is that the Igbo, Hausas, Yoruba's, and other tribes need each other and in my own thinking, they need us more.

- Even if we separate into many countries, we still need each other.

- The biggest problem in Nigeria is the inability to understand and accept each other the way God created us.

- If we remain a united country, we will be able to tap from the diverse blessings that God gave to each section.

- No country on earth can operate in isolation; each still needs the other for better functioning and operation.

- Nigeria is like our natural body and any wrong adjustment, constitutional manipulation without amendment will disorganize us and affect our progress the more.

- The choice has been made, what we need is the training so that each part can function at its best.

- There are things each tribe are best known for, and once discovered, must be perfected.

- It is the duty of the whole parts to contribute and help each other until perfection.

- If we train hands to do the work of the feet, train the feet to do the work of the ears, and challenge the eyes to function in place of the mouth, the final result will be FAILURE and INEFFECTIVENESS. This is the Nigerian position now.

- The Igbo are very good in many aspects in life. They are greatly gifted and mightily talented in many areas of life.

- A primary school leaver from Igbo tribe can comfortably compete with any graduate in every area in any part of the world.

- They are equally gifted in developing cities and nations.

- They are so enterprising, well informed and good in taking up challenges.

- They are very scientific in nature.

- In the area of business, academic, social life, management, leadership, etc., they are the best.

- Talking about business, trading or starting from nobody to somebody, they are the best.

- The only problem is that they use their best outside Igbo land.

- To develop our land, we want the co-operation of the Federal Government and the other tribes of Nigeria.

- This is the only time we are coming out, asking for help and support from Nigeria after the civil war.

- After the civil war, the displaced Igbo were not helped.

- Our money in the banks was seized. We lost our properties in every city.

- Our children were out of school for three years.

- Our farms were invaded by Nigerian soldiers; our children were raped and elders were slapped and insulted before their children.

- Our businesses were destroyed.

- The 144 and 138 Battalion of Nigerian army particularly in my town Agbogugu committed a lot of atrocities. I do not want to go into details, but my town up till now has not been compensated and we still need to be compensated.

- Millions of Igbo were starved and they died without help from anyone. This is the reason why some Igbo went into crimes to succeed. If we treat the present displaced Nigerian northeast the same way, the Boko Haram will equip them to greater crimes. Everyone has a role to play to settle the displaced in the world.

- We acknowledge and accept that our functions are different. We are not in competition with any tribe because we know that evil competition brings conflicts and failure.

- Co-operation with Nigeria will lead us to finish the task before us in good time.

- God has made each tribe what they are today; unique, different, and necessary.

- Though we come from different tribes, we are the same nation.

- I really support the emergency of Biafra and the youths under agitation if it's God's will/time but as a minister, I need to go into spiritual warfare to make it happen timely and to the glory of God.

WHAT TO DO TO SUCCEED

- There must be harmony, unity, and the head must not disregard the hand nor does the hand neglect the eyes (1 Corinthians 12:14-17).

- We must love one another, help one another, care for one another, and work in unity.

- If the intestines begin to struggle to come out so that it can be seen like the eyes, the whole body will be in trouble and even die.

- So, wherever you find yourself, remain there and function effectively.

- I have said before in my book, ***The Fall and the Rise of Igbo Nation*** that we want to industrialize Igbo land like China and build it like Dubai.

DEMANDS FROM THE SEAT OF POWER IN ABUJA AND IGBO LEADERS

- Maximum security in Igbo land

- Uninterrupted power supply

- Proper dredging of River Nigeria to accommodate bigger cargo ships boarding at Onitsha and Uguta sea port to international level.

- Access road to the centre of industry and unity, and federal government roads in Igbo land well maintained.

- Branches of all foreign embassies in Nigeria located to Igbo land.

- Proposal should be written and given to the national assembly and the presidency for immediate implementation.

- The Igbo want to build industry in the centre of unity, in Igbo land that connects other Igbo states.

- The Igbo want to build special schools in Igbo land.

- The Igbo want to build 5-star hotels in Igbo land.

- One more State to be created in Igbo land.

- Nigerian business people, we want them to help in developing Igbo land.

- Foreign investors, we want foreign investors to be attracted to Igbo land.

CHAPTER14

BRING BACK YOUR MONEY

— (EXODUS 10:24-26; 12:31-36)

- My plea to Igbo leaders who have bank accounts outside is to bring back the money to start something in Igbo land.

- The migration of money capital is a transfer of money that can be used to develop Igbo land than a foreign land.

- Such money is being used to develop industries, technology, and agriculture that we import.

- Your money outside is being used to start ndustries, employ their citizens, make life comfortable, and produce goods they sell to us here.

- If you bring your money back and open up factories, you can employ our jobless youths, reduce the rate of poverty and crime, and you will make more people useful and reasonable.

- It is occultism that makes people think only about their families. That is why some people will take their money abroad and save it in a bank for the future use of their children at the expenses of millions of others.

- Most of that money after death is lost to the benefit of the Western world.

- With the security in Igbo land, power, and development, your money is more protected here than any other place.

- Your money can create jobs for hundreds of people. Poverty, crimes, and wickedness drive and sustain their stronghold in any place where there is no job.

- A single industry can bring joy, peace, blessings, and hope in a person's family and a city to your credit.

- If you have vision and passion for the development of Igbo nation, you will not keep money in any bank if it can be used to open an industry and deliver people from suffering.

- The accumulation of African leaders' money in British banks help them to keep great number of their citizens in jobs, pay their bills, and help the country to remain great economically.

- Some of the researches, technologies, and development in the Western world are being funded by the gains from the mineral resources from Africa.

- The Igbo have that capacity to develop scientifically and develop technologies that can be the pride of Africa.

- Igbo have the intellectual capital that can produce persons like Bill Gates, Stephen Jobs, Henry Ford (the founder of CNN), Michael Dell (the founder of DELL computers), Richard Branson (the founder of Virgin Atlantic), Thomas Edison (the founder of General Electric), just to mention but a few.

- Our son, Philip Emeagwalu, an Igbo born, migrated to America can give the Igbo the best computer university in Africa that will compete with the best in the world if he is sure of our support and security.

- Adiche Chimamanda, with high level intellectual capital can give us the best university in her area of discipline if she is sure of the security of her life. Ngozi Okonjo Iweala can do more.

- These and more Igbo who migrated to developed world can convert their intellectual capital into products, service, and wealth if they can be supported financially.

- If you bring back your money, Igbo have enough people with intellectual capital that can give us enough information, knowledge, technology, agriculture, and companies that can transform Igbo land like the best cities in the world.

- The primary determinant of development, wealth, and greatness is intellectual capital. But we need money to affect that.

- Brains can be used to take money from countries that have oil, diamond, gold and other mineral resources, and be richer than those countries.

- Igbo nation is full of men and women with such brains. If you bring back your money and support Igbo brainy born, they will give us the technology that will gather the wealth of the world.

- This is because technological superiority outpaces all the mineral resources of countries without intellectual capital.

- The intellectual capital of Bill Gates, founder of Microsoft, earns him $500 every second many years ago.

- In contrast, half of the world's population which is about three billion lives on the average of $500 a month.

- Some of these people are from Nigeria, Saudi Arabia, Venezuela, other OPEC countries and they have oil.

- Bill Gates' technological discovery taxes computer users in the world and he is richer than 70 nations in the world put together.

- If you bring your money back, Igbo has more brainy people than many countries in the world.

- Igbo has many people in Igbo land with high level of intellectual capital who are being wasted because of lack of support.

- I am sure that, if you bring your money back and invest it in the development of the Igbo land, there will be development.

- The intellectual Igbo people if developed can enter into every part of the world and share with their wealth.

- An intelligent person can use his intelligence to rule the world.

- Many nations in the world over the years are using their intellectual capitals to exploit more than 40% of Nigerian oil field.

- How? Because they have the technology we do not have.

- They tax Nigeria to bring out their crudes from the oil field and charge us 40%.

- The remaining 60%, Nigeria use part of the money to export the crude to those nations and after refining, they sell the oil to us at a very high price.

- The reason is because we do not have the technology to refine our crude, or that we refuse to.

- I think what the Igbo are supposed to fight for more is how to develop Igbo land, and develop our scientists who are wasting.

- Our governors if use the state allocation well can develop our land.

- Am not sure that the Niger Delta who have the oil field that feed Nigeria is the richest in Nigeria. Why? Because of under development and ignorance.

- Unfortunately, the people that would have developed Igbo land, Niger Delta, and Nigeria as a whole are frustrated outside or inside.

- Countries are praying and looking for the service of the Like of Bath Nnaji, but Nigeria ignored him.

- Intelligence leads to scientific discoveries and can be used to capture the mineral resources of a whole nation.

- Before, Ghanaians, many African countries come to study in Nigeria, but recently, half of Nigerian students are in Ghana because we fail to develop our educational system.

- In the old days, Nigerians who go to study in America come back to work after their studies. But the reverse is the case today; they stay back to work, especially the intelligent ones.

- This is what is called, flight of intelligent capital. This is the brain or intelligence that is meant to develop our land but they stay back. It is the migration of intelligence.

- They work and use their intelligence capital to produce job, service, and comfort for people in those countries. It is called brain drain.

- Instead of looking inside and developing the brainy people in Niger Delta, they prefer small tokens from the Federal Government.

- The Igbo allow their brainy people escape, kidnap them, kill some, and make others afraid from coming home to develop their land.

- The Western world in turn, employs the few escaped ones like Philip Emeagwalu, Chimamanda, and many others.

- In return, they use their brain in exchange of their knowledge and pay them salaries.

- Even the salary they receive, they are taxed to take almost their salaries under merciless bills called policies.

- Natural resources, having oil field, gold, etc., are not as important as having knowledge.

- The West come here, take our crude oil, raw materials, sell our oil to us, use our raw material to make shoes, tooth picks, clothes, and sell to us because of lack of intelligent capital (Lamentation 5:4-8).

- Africa and Igbo in particular, who have men and women of knowledge are living at the mercy of others because of our inability to develop technologically.

- It is a pity that the Igbo who developed *Ogbunigwe* bomb that disorganized Nigerian Army have joined other parts of Nigeria to struggle over paper certificate.

- We must come back to technology. We can compete with them in both, but must not abandon what we are born to do, technologically knowhow. We must discover what we are created to discover to help the world.

CHAPTER 15

UNDER-DEVELOPED IGBO NATION

- When the children of Israel were permitted by a decree to go back and develop their land (Ezra 1:1-11), only 42,360 caught the vision (Ezra 2:64, 65). The majority of the people preferred their business, houses, and gardens in foreign land, Babylon, to the desolation of their land. Only the poor went with Zerubbabel, and they really suffered building the temple (Ezra 4:1-6).

- I was talking with one Northern Nigerian man sometimes ago before the last election in 2015. He was an M.D in one of the ministries in Nigeria. I was surprised by what he told me at that time. The country was in the verge of breaking, if not Jonathan's action by accepting defeat.

My findings:

- I discovered that the North is ready for Separation if worst comes to worst.

- From what he told me, everything that will keep the north to stand and develop as a country is already in place.

- Almost all the modern equipment for farming is in place, waiting for the nation's separation to be put to use.

- There are other mineral resources discovered in the north which are still untouched.

- The West also has a lot of untapped mineral resources and they are ready for separation, though they are not making any noise.

- Only the uninformed, jobless Igbo and possibly homeless Igbo are making noise, yet they are the only ones who are underdeveloped. Ask the law materials and mineral research in Nigeria to prove this claim.

- The Northern Nigeria agriculture if put into use can feed the whole West Africa.

- The West is also working with the fast growth of Lagos, agriculture and their maritime industry, well established.

- The city of Lagos alone is richer than many countries in Africa. Few persons in some offices in Lagos with a single policy take money from the account of all the Igbo in Lagos to furnish the state treasury.

- The entire big time Igbo importers are controlled by policies that take their money all over the nation.

- As their business grows the state and federal treasuries increases. That is normal, but the Igbo are the target. At a stage, their business comes to a halt.

- Recently, the West decided to develop Lagos to a modern city. Tejuosho market was affected, others market in Lagos were included.

- In all this, Igbo traders are always the victims. The Ladipo market in Mushin was given some days to leave. All this place is occupied by Igbo traders.

- If you do not look into the matter very well, you will think or conclude that Igbo are being marginalized, but the truth is that, they want to develop Lagos and you cannot blame them.

- The only problem was that alternative is not always provided. This always put the Igbo out of job, but it is not anyone's fault because cities must be developed.

- Very soon, agriculture will compete or do better than the oil in Nigeria.

- The west already can survive without any other tribe because they are developed maritime wise.

- The only people that will suffer are the Igbo, because they have not developed their land.

- Therefore, those Igbo who are fighting for Biafra are not informed or well educated. You are agitating for Biafra but even a blind but a wise Nigeria knows that this country is tribally centralized.

- Other tribes are preparing to survive alone in case of pronounced separation, expect the Igbo.

- This is because the Igbo' investments are outside their land.

- All that has happened to Igbo in the North, West, and other parts of Nigeria in times of crisis is enough to move the Igbo to develop their land.

- However, because the problems of the Igbo are spiritual like I have said, they don't have the will power to do so.

- Most people who are clamoring for Biafra have no place to stay if they are asked to leave. We must start preparing for the above with wisdom.

- You may quote the United Nations law that permit you to own property in any part of the world but that has never worked in any nation where there were crises, even the Biafra war time and after.

- Do not be deceived, we are not ready for Biafra, though we really need it. Other parts of Nigeria are more ready than us.

- To be sincere, the only thing holding Nigeria today as a country is the oil, take oil away and the Nigeria will disintegrate and the Igbo will suffer most.

CHAPTER 16

OCCULTISM, ENEMY OF DEVELOPMENT

— (ACTS 16:16, 19)

WHAT IS OCCULTISM?

- Occultism is satanic operation shut off from view or exposure to the general public.

- Occultism is an unrevealed activity of the devil to non-members.

- Occultism is satanic secret made known to people who are in covenant with him.

- It is an action of wickedness not easily apprehended or understood by non-members.

- Occultism is obtuse, mysterious, hidden from view, and concealed from public consumption.

- Occultism is an action from the dark world not detectable by clinical methods most times.

- It is an evil act made unavailable in macroscopic amount.

- Occultism is an evil involvement with supernormal power or some secret knowledge of the devil.

- It is an evil action lost to notice against victim.

- It is an evil action or influence of supernatural or supernormal powers designed to waste lives and properties.

- Occultism is seeking information or helps from evil spirits (Daniel 2:1-3, 10-11).

- Occultism is sacrifice to the devil, divination, use of charms, or being a necromancer (Deuteronomy 18:9-12; 2 Kings 2:1, 2; 1 Chronicles 10:13, 14; Acts 8:9-11; 16:16-19; Revelation 21:8).

THE DEVIL AND OCCULTISM

- The devil and the Anti-Christ are the head of occultism and demonic intelligence (Exodus 7:10-13, 20-22; 8:5-7, 20-23; 1 Samuel 18:10, 11).

- The devil is presently using occultism to destroy the world.

- It is dangerous to combine intelligence with occult practices. It will bring confusion and foolishness (Romans 1:18-32).

- No nation will succeed or remain great with occultism (Daniel 8:23; Ezekiel 28:6; 2 Thessalonians 2:7-12; Revelation 13:11-17).

- Occultism makes people foolish, selfish, wicked, brutal, and unreasonable (Daniel 2:13, 14).

- An occult person is cruel, suicidal, and mad in disappointment in times of failure (Daniel 6:4-9, 15-17).

- Occultism and intelligence without God are against true development.

- Intelligence comes from God, but if the benefactor refuses to surrender his life to God, through Christ, he will be corrupted, deceived, and brought to vanity (Ezekiel 28:1-19; Psalm 39:5).

- Intelligence capital without God and Christ His son will lead to doom.

- America is struggling economically today because they ignored God. Their prosperity was rooted in the relationship their ancestors had with God. But today, they are going down because of their backsliding.

- In 1609 when their pilgrims left Scrooby, England, they established a Christian nation.

- George Washington who is known as the father of America in his speech said in his last address to the congress, "It is impossible to rightly govern the world without God and the Bible."

- It is impossible to govern the universe without the aid of Supreme Being.

- Not only in America, the whole world today had problems with governance because of backsliding.

- The root of backsliding is traced to idolatry and occultism.

- The world leaders have mixed intelligence with occultism.

- So, if Igbo land must be developed, our leaders and all the Igbo have to separate our God-given intelligence from occultism (Numbers 13:27; Deuteronomy 29:29).

- I am sure that Igbo land is filled with a lot of blessing, milk and honey. The secret things belong to God and if we can only go to God, He will open our intelligent brain, scientific eyes to see hidden blessings that are more profitable than oil.

- God will use Igbo scientists to discover great mineral resources in the world.

- I believe that more than 90% percent of good things in the whole earth are yet to be discovered. Civilization in our society is still very small.

- Because of man's gross ignorance of God, the world's best mineral resources or deposits are yet to be discovered (Psalm 12:1; Isaiah 64:4).

- There are natural unseen gates, doors leading to God's blessings yet to be found. Oil, gold, diamond, etc., cannot stabilize global economic crisis (Psalm 24:6, 7).

- Our world is still grossly underdeveloped. No matter what you think America and other developed countries have achieved, they are little compared to what our God has prepared for us.

- The little technology that is revealed has made men to abandon God.

- God needs the best brains and the best minds to bring more development to the world.

- He used Daniel and his colleagues in Babylon to develop that nation.

- Moses discovered his spiritual capital. He was both intelligent and spiritual. With his opportunity for formal education, he was mightily used of God.

- Paul's knowledge of Greek helped him to be accepted among the scholars or university students in Mars Hills, an academy where Plato had taught; a city where Socrates lived and died, where Aristotle had both learned and taught. Prominent philosophers of Paul's days, the Epicureans and Stoics were ministered to by Paul in their language.

- Luke, Paul's companion who was a medical doctor also was greatly used (Colossians 4:14).

- Demas, Martin Luther, John Wesley, Whitefield, Charles Finny, and David Living Stone (a medical doctor) were mightily used. This is combined intelligence with spiritual capital.

- Spiritual capital can lead you to intellectual knowledge and discovery.

- God is not looking for demonically intelligent, worldly wise, brilliantly cunning, treacherous, power drunk personality, and dangerous geniuses.

- He is tired of people whose lives are characterized by pride, perversion, conflicts, and deceits.

- These kinds of intelligent ones are subtle, wicked, and being used by the devil to intimidate, persecute and to destroy God's ordained laws.

- These evil leaders have filled the nations of the world with sin, possessed by the devil, lazy spirits, unproductive sexual demons; selfish, careless, and indifferent youth and retired evil elders, senior citizens assigned to destroy divine standards.

- God is looking for intelligent, educated and Spirit-controlled, excellent leaders whom He will anoint to develop cities to His glory.

- He is looking for the rich or poor, who will submit for His empowerment, to excel among others to develop cities.

- He is looking for humble people from any background, to anoint and empower to separate for city development.

- He is looking for the best or worst of human beings who will surrender to His leadership and will be distinguished and empowered to develop cities.

- If you are ready, the only thing you need is to repent, confess your sins, and ask for divine empowerment.

- No matter how low or high you are, if you surrender to God for Igbo development, He will make you exceptional; first among your equals, superior, unsurpassed, and valuable for city development.

- If you are ready, then you have to be strong in the Lord, not in yourself, occultism, witchcraft, or any other means.

CHAPTER 17

MOURNING FOR IGBO NATION

" All of them also ate the same spiritual food and drank the same spiritual drink, which flowed from the spiritual rock that followed them. That rock was Christ."

— (1 CORINTHIANS 10:3-5).

- Daniel in his book, Chapter twenty-one, was about 90 years of age and was no longer active in public service when he wrote that chapter (Daniel 10:1; 1:21; 9:1, 2).

- Daniel was a man of understanding in spiritual matters who was involved in captivity and monitored the prophecies, timing, and prayed for the manifestation (Jeremiah 25:8-14; Ezra 1:1-11).

- King Cyrus, which some suspect to be Queen Esther's son made a decree that the children of Judah could go back to their land (Isaiah 45:1-1-7).

- Surprisingly, many were not interested to return back after seventy years of captivity.

- Only 42, 360 returned with determination to build the temple and the city (Ezra 2:64, 65; 4:1-6).

- The great number of the people, scientists, business, and wealthy ones preferred their beautiful houses and gardens in Babylon to the abandoned and desolation of their home land, which is the same with the Igbo today.

- The few that went back under the leadership of Zerubbabel had much difficulty and opposition in building the temple and the city.

- Almost all the rich Igbo people who are comfortable outside Igbo land despise the call to develop the land.

- In the time of Daniel, he was disappointed and sorrowful for the nonchalant attitude of the wealthy Jews.

- His worry and concern increased and moved him to mourn towards heaven because of the few Jews who had gone to Judah and the Jews who were not interested in the restoration of Jerusalem and building the temple (Daniel 10:1-3).

- He started fasting and praying on the 3rd of Nisan and the answer through the heavenly visitors came on the 24th of the month of Nisan.

- His prayer concentrated on the forgiveness of the children of Israel, the fulfilment of Jeremiah's prophecy, and the development of the Jews (Daniel 10:12, 14; 9:24; 12:1).

- Daniel knew that the time appointed by God for the deliverance of the children of Israel has come. He prayed and fasted for three full weeks, mourning towards heaven.

- Igbo should dedicate all their sit at home for prayers in designated places in every community, cities and villages for the liberation of Igbo nation.

- We need spiritual leaders who can interpret the signs, bend the mind of people and move the Igbo into action.

- The Scriptures rightly said that where there is no vision, people perish.

- We need to do something to develop our land and to save our born and unborn children from perishing.

- Pharaoh may be behind us with all his soldiers who are trained to kill; the Red Sea may be raging ahead of us; there may be lions in the forests; serpents, wall of Jericho's, Balaam's, Barak's, witches, and wizards, with all the nations on our way. But our God wants us to develop the Igbo land (Joshua 7:5-16).

- Whenever the children of Israel suffered loss, entered into problems, it is the leaders that normally enter into prayers and mourn towards heaven until restoration takes place.

- David besought God, prayed, and mourned towards heaven when his child became sick. He lay all night upon the earth for seven days mourning without food.

- Esther and Mordecai mourned and fasted for three days and nights to reverse the evil decrees against the Jews.

- Believers and leaders of the Igbo must not give up in prayer and fasting, mourning towards heaven until our people are liberated.

- When Daniel started his prayers, mourning for the children of Israel, it was not easy for him.

- The prince of the kingdom of Persia withstood him for twenty-one days, trying to discourage him. His spiritual and physical strength was attacked, but he refused to give up.

- The prince of the kingdom of Persia who withstood God's angelic messenger was the satanic prince or ruler of the kingdom of Persia.

- This ruler of darkness was determined to keep the children of Israel in captivity for life, but Daniel confronted them.

- Igbo spiritual leaders must come out to mourn towards heaven, and confront the powers of darkness holding Igbo nation down.

- The liberation of the Igbo race will not be achieved without confronting the spiritual forces responsibly (Daniel 10:12, 13; John 12:31).

- If the prince in charge of the case file of Igbo nation is not cast out, every other effort will not yield any good result.

- Every problem has spirit or spirits in charge of them, and as long as the spirits are not dealt with, other things will end in frustration (Luke 11:21, 22).

- Igbo needs help from heaven, to receive divine might to be free from her bondage.

- The Prince of Grecian referred to in Daniel 10:20, is also a demon and once in position, her captives must keep suffering.

- No person, family, or nation can succeed without the help from God, and this help can only come when some powers are dislodged.

- Satan through an organized network of principalities, powers, spiritual wickedness and rulers of darkness can hold a person, people, and nations in bondage when they are not confronted.

- They can hinder people and stop them from fulfilling God's purpose and plan on earth.

- Igbo need help from above to reclaim their place in life and achieve her greatness in the nation (Daniel 10:14-21).

- This is an urgent call for every Igbo person, especially our spiritual leaders and the intercessors to shun every other thing, set time apart, mourn, pray, and fast to ask help from God, and the time is now.

- Having an Igbo President just for eight years is not enough, we need prayers for Igbo liberation.

CHAPTER 18

BE STRONG IN THE LORD

— (ACTS 19:21-41; EPHESIANS 6:10)

THE SOURCE OF OUR POWER

— GOD'S WORD (ACTS 6:7. 12:19-20, 24).

THE CAUSE OF RIOT

- Blind zeal in false religion (John 16:1-3).

- Personal prejudice and envy (Matthew 27:17-23).

- Ignorance and foolishness (Acts 19:32).

- Loss of unlawful gain (Acts16:16-22).

- Materialism (Acts 19:23-28).

- The church in Ephesus was founded by Paul. Aquila, Priscilla, and Apollos were used mightily to the growth of the believers.

- Paul spent three years ministering at Ephesus and when he left, he instructed Timothy to take up the leadership of the church.

- Pergamos was the official capital of Asia Minor but Ephesus was the greatest city.

- A Roman historian called Ephesus "the light of Asia".

- Ephesus has the greatest harbour in Asia Minor.

- It was a very important place for commerce.

- Ephesus was called the market place of Asia.

- It was also the place for big games and many people came to Ephesus for the games from different parts of Asia.

- Ephesus was the Centre for the worship of the goddess, Diana.

- Her temple was one of the seven wonders of the ancient world.

- Sale of idols was big business in Ephesus.

- In the temple, little gods were sold to all the idol worshippers for so much money.

- Ephesus was dominated by the practices of witchcraft and all manner of occultism, just like our nation Nigeria.

- Those who were strong those days got their power from Ephesus.

- Many were strong in embezzling public fund, killing people, kidnapping, wasting destinies, and bewitchment.

- Ephesus produced many occult groups; occult grand masters who were making gains by destroying people's destinies, just like Nigeria (Acts 16:16, 19).

- When Paul saw how deceived they were by believing that none could succeed without being strong in occult, he wrote a letter to them (Ephesians 6:10).

- We are living in a time when people believe that nobody can be rich or rise to certain position in life without belonging to the cult.

It is a lie and deceit of the devil.

- Others may believe this and may even prosper that way, but Igbo is not destined to serve idol, prosper in the occult and yet build their city.

- If you must build your city, contribute in developing Igbo land, you need to be strong in the Lord, not in occult, witchcraft, wickedness, or destruction.

- Many Igbo who prospered in Ogboni and other occult (idol worshippers) prospered in the expense of their children, parents, brothers and sisters.

- For many of them, their families are suffering and there is no hope of survival outside Christ (Lamentation 5:7).

- Any Igbo person that wants to be strong in prosperity, wealth, richness or politics must find the Lord Jesus Christ.

- It is a deceit to believe that you can be strong in the Lord at the same time in the occult.

- Going to church, building churches, or belonging to a strong group in any church is different from being strong in the Lord.

- You can be a pope, a knight, a priest, a bishop, or hold any title on earth, but if you are not born again, you are not strong.

- You may be strong academically, politically, financially, materially, etc., but if you are not born again, you are not strong.

- Your strength is useless, unprofitable, and as good as an empty barrel if you are not born again.

- I have carefully studied the beginning of occultism, idolatry, wickedness, and their end.

■ I have lived long to prove that being strong without God is worse than useless and lighter than emptiness, nothing.

CHAPTER 19

DIFFERENT REWARDS

THE REWARDS OF THE WICKED

— (PSALM 1:4-6)

- A wicked person is like chaff, a tree without root or fruit and will not be able to stand in the Day of Judgment.

- The wicked are troubled, restless, and are burdened.

- An evil doer and a wicked person shall be cut off.

- The axe of justice shall fall on the wicked.

- The riches of the wicked shall melt away, his power will decay and their joy shall be turned to sorrow.

- Their house and chair of office shall be empty, and their estate without an owner.

- The name of the wicked shall be blotted out and brought to the deathbed of penury.

- The wicked shall be gone like a passing cloud and forgotten as dream.

- They will not see how close their destruction is.

- They may be having feast days with no safe days.

- The only one choice left for the wicked is to repent or burn forever in Hell. They are cursed on a daily basis.

THE REWARDS OF THE RIGHTEOUS

- True happiness is only found in doing the right things; doing the things God prospers.

- The righteous prospers and is happy (Job 17:9).

- No matter how long it takes, it shall be well with the righteous (Psalm 23:4-6).

- God pays back everything in folds.

- The saints are preserved forever (Psalm 37:23-26).

- The Lord will not leave the righteous in the hand of the wicked.

- The righteous will have everlasting satisfaction.

- The eyes of the Lord, His face, ears, presence and power are all engaged actively to help, heal, sustain, support, protect, and preserve all that trust in Him.

- Strength, happiness, answers to prayers, and long quality life belong to the upright.

- As for the wicked, disappointments, sorrows, destructions, and untimely deaths awaits the unrighteous.

- Finally, each part you take, leads to a destination (Romans 5:20). God may not stop problems, trials or temptation from coming to you, but He has provided a way out. Let us join hands to build the Igbo land. God bless you.

FINAL REWARDS

- The overcomer's crown, an incorruptible crown (1 Corinthians 9:25).

- The crown of glory for feeding the flock of God (1Peter 5:4).

- Crown of righteousness, for loving His appearance (2 Timothy 4:8).

- The soul winners crown, crown of rejoicing (1Thessalonians 2:19; Daniel 12:3).

- The crown of life, for tried, and triumphant saints (James 1:12).

CHAPTER 20

CHURCH AGE AND ESCHATALOGY

- Eschatology is a branch of theology concerned with the final events in the history of the world or of mankind.

- It is a belief concerning death, the end of the world, or the ultimate destiny of mankind.

- The church age or the last days is the characteristics of the present happenings to prove that the end is at hand - 2 Timothy 3:1-5.

- In the past, it is called the age or the ages to come - Ephesians 2:7; Hebrews 6:5.1.

CHARACTERISTICS OF THE PRESENT AGE

- The last times or later days – 1 Peter 1:5; 1 John 2:18; Daniel 10:14; Deuteronomy 4:30; Isaiah 2:2; Micah 4:1.

- A period of time marked by dominion of Satan - 2 Corinthians 4:4.

- A period of time marked by denial of True God - Luke 17:26; 2 Timothy 3:4-5.

- A period of time marked by evil activities - Galatians 1:4.

- A period of time marked by the denial of Christian living - 2 Timothy 3:1-8; Jude 18.

- A period of time marked by the denial of sound doctrines - 2 Timothy 4:3-4.

- A period of time marked by denial of true faith - 1 Timothy 4:1-4; Jude 3.

- A period of time marked by denial of Christ - 1 John 2:18; 4:3; 2 Peter2:15.

- A period of time marked by denial of authority - 2 Timothy 3:4.

- A period of time marked by denial of Christ's return - 2 Peter 3:3-4.

- A Period of time marked by ungodliness, darkness, and lusts - Ephesians 6:12; 2:2; 1 Corinthians 2:6-7; Titus 2:12

BELIEVERS RESPONSBILITY

Genesis 19:12-17; Matthew 28:18-20; Mark 16:15, 16; Acts 1:4, 8, 13, 14; 8:1-4; John 4:35-38; 9:1-4; Revelation 22:12-17.

- Preaching to others at every opportunity is every believer's responsibility. It is a debt you owe everyone you can reach physically, through social media, and any given opportunity - Romans 16:17; Proverbs 19:27.

- Living a holy life - Hebrews 12:14; 1 John 3:1-3; Luke 21:34-36.

- Loving God with jealousy - Philippians 3:7-21; Titus 2:11-14.

This is not the time to compete with the world because the time is very dangerous. It is a time to be serious with evangelism because disaster is taking place without much notice or signs (1 Corinthians 7:29-31).

- It is a time to separate from the corrupt worldly system to avoid the coming trouble (Jeremiah 30:7).

CHAPTER 21

THE RAPTURE OF THE SAINTS

HOW IT WILL HAPPEN

- Just as Elijah, Enoch, and Noah were taken away to safety in the times of troubles so also the saints, true believers who are born again, living a holy life at the moment of rapture, will be translated to meet the Lord in the air.

- You remember that at the time of flood, Noah escaped and Lot escaped the judgment of fire on Sodom and Gomorrah. That is how the saints will be raptured (1 Thessalonians 4:13-18; John 14:1-3; 1 Corinthians 15:23, 51-58; Luke 21:34-36).

THE TRUTH ABOUT THE RAPTURE

- All the prophecies that must be fulfilled before the rapture takes place are being fulfilled right before us now - Matthew 24:37-39; 1 Timothy 4:1-3; 2 Timothy 3:1-5; Acts 2:17-18; 3:20-21; 2 Peter 3:3-4.

- If you are not ready for the rapture now, you are deceived and you have put yourself in danger of troubles that is about to start - Jeremiah 30:7.

- Rapture means the catching up of all truly born-again Christians to meet the Lord in the air.

- It is a time when Christ comes for the saints.

- At rapture, Christ does not appear visibly to those on the earth. He only appears in the air to resurrect the true saints who have died, change the living saints and catch them up to meet the Lord in the air.

- It will take place in a moment of time, in the twinkling of an eye – 1 Corinthians 15:23, 51-58; Philippians 3:20-21; 1 Thessalonians 4:13-17.

- We shall be changed and caught up; transformed and translated - Genesis 5:24; Hebrews 11:5; 2 Kings 2:11-12; Acts 1:9-11.

THE REASON FOR THE RAPTURE

■ To raise the saints who have died (1 Thessalonians 4:13-16; 1 Corinthians 15:21-23, 51-58; Revelation 20:4-6).

■ To transform the bodies of living saints who are holy at that moment from mortality to immortality (1 Corinthians 15:51-58; Philippians 3:20-21; 2 Corinthians 5:1-8).

■ To remove all the saints out of this world before the great tribulation (1 Thessalonians 4:13-17; Luke 21:34-36; 2 Thessalonians 2:1, 7-8; Genesis 19:12-17).

■ To take the saints as His inheritance forever (John 14:1-3; 1 Thessalonians 4:17; Ephesians 5:27; 2 Thessalonians 2:1).

■ To bring all the saints together for the marriage supper of the lamb and give them rewards for their work (Revelation 19:1-11; 2 Corinthians 5:8-10).

QUALIFICATION TO BE RAPTURED

■ To be raptured, you have to maintain a holy walk with Christ all the time, especially at the time of rapture.

■ To be raptured, you have to be holy and maintain good relationship with God at the time of death - Amos 4:12.

- To be raptured, you have to be steadfast, unmovable, and working for God - 1 Corinthians 15:58; Revelation 2:26; 3:11.

- Rapture is different from the Second Advent or second coming of Christ - Zacharias 14:1-5; Jude14; Revelation 19:11-21.

- Second coming is the time Christ comes to the earth with the saints. The rapture can take place any moment, any time from now because we are living in the last days of this age. If you are not ready to meet the Lord now, you are in a fearful position and in a terrible mess.

CHAPTER 22

THE JUDGMENT SEAT OF GOD OR BEMA

— 2 CORINTHIANS 5:1-10; ROMANS 14:10-12; 1 CORINTHIANS 3:6-15; REVELATION 19:7-8

THE JUDGMENT EXPLAINED

- Immediately after the rapture, two programs will take place at the same time.

- The first one is referred to as appearing before the judgment seat of Christ. This judgment is for believers and it is not a time to consider his salvation or question it. Every sinful question is settled before rapture - Romans 8:1; John 5:24; 1 John 4:17.

- The purpose of this judgment is to examine believers work and know how to reward him - 2 Corinthians 5:1-10.

- After the *bema* judgment and reward receiving, there will be marriage with Christ, called the ***Marriage Supper of the Lamb*** - Revelation 19:7-8.

- The meaning of judgment seat of Christ explained in: 2 Corinthians 5:10; Romans 14:10.

- The Greek word is **"bema"** translated judgment seat meaning; reward seat.

- The time of the bema judgment of Christ - Luke 14:12-14; 1 Corinthians 4:5; 2 Timothy 4:8; Revelation 22:12.

- The place the judgment reward will take place is in the air, heavenly place, in the presence of God - 1 Thessalonians 4:17; 2 Corinthians 5:1-8.

- Jesus Christ is going to be the judge during the bema reward 2 Corinthians 5:10; John 5:22; Romans 14:10; Revelation 2:7, 17, 25-28; 3:12, 21; 22:12-16.

- He will give believers rewards according to their works.

- Every believers' work shall be tested by fire - 1 Corinthians 3:8-15.

- Some shall suffer loss, which is loss of rewards; others will receive reward 1 Corinthians 3:13-15.

TYPES OF REWARDS

- The soul winner's reward is crown of rejoicing - 1 Thessalonians 2:19; Daniel 12:3.

- The overcomers' reward is incorruptible crown - 1 Corinthians 9:25.

- The crown of life, for tested, tried, and triumphant saints - James 1:12.

- The crown of glory, for feeding the flock of God - 1 Peter 5:4.

- The crown of righteousness, for loving His appearance - 2 Timothy 4:8.

- The kind of rewards you receive determines where you will seat before the marriage commences.

THE PROPER MARRIGE; THE MARRIAGE OF THE LAMB

<u>(John 3:29; Romans 7:4; 2 Corinthians 11:2; Ephesians 5:25-33; Revelation 19:7, 8; 21:1-22)</u>).

- This marriage will bring the true church and believers into an eternal union with Christ. It will take place between the *bema* rewards and the second advent of Christ.

- **Jesus Christ is the bridegroom** - Revelation 19:7; Matthew 9:14-15; John 3:27-30; 2 Corinthians 11:2; Ephesians 5:25-27, 32.

- **The bride of the Lamb** - Revelation 19:7-8; 2 Corinthians 11:2; Ephesians 5:25-27, 30-32. The church will be the bride because the church is the chaste virgin, presented to Christ while Israel will be restored - 2 Corinthians 11:2. The dress of the Bride is Righteousness - Revelation 19:8; Ephesians 5:25-27; 2 Corinthians 11:2.

- **Who are the blessed guests of the Lamb?** - Revelation 19:9-10; John 3:28-29; Luke 13:28-29. The saints of the Old Testament, believers, martyred during the Tribulation, end time redeemed Israel, and Gentiles apart from the church form the invited guests - Revelation 6:9-11.

CHAPTER 23

GREAT TRIBULATION

- General tribulation is the common problem that everyone on earth goes through [John 15:18-21; 16:33; Matthew 13:20, 21; Acts 14:21, 22; Romans 5:1-5; 8:35-39; 12:12; 2 Corinthians 1:3, 4; 7:4; Ephesians 3:12, 13; 1 Thessalonians 3:1-4; Revelation 1:9; 2:9].

- Great Tribulation will occur after the rapture, and will take time at the same time with the *bema* judgment in different places.

- During this time, the Antichrist will take possession of this world for the reign of terror.

- He will be a system or organization, but also a person; a supernatural, diabolical being in the form of a man who will blaspheme and proclaim himself to be God - Daniel 8:23-

25; 2 Thessalonians 2:7-12; Revelation 13:1-18; Jeremiah 30:5-7, 11-11; Daniel 9:27; 12:1; Matthew 24:3-38.

THE NATURE OF GREAT TRIBULATION

- It will be a time of Trouble - Jeremiah 30:7; Zephaniah 1:14, 15; Daniel 12:1.

- It will be a time of wrath - Zephaniah 1:15, 18; 1 Thessalonians 1:10; 5:9; Revelation 6:16, 17. 11:18; 14:10, 19; 15:1, 7; 16:1, 19.

- It will be a time of judgment - Revelation 14:7; 15:4; 16:5, 7; 19:2.

- It will be a time of trial - Revelation 3:10.

- It will be a time of desolation - Daniel 9:27; Zephaniah 1:14, 15.

- It will be a time of indignation - Isaiah 26:20, 21; 34:13.

- It will be a time of overturning - Isaiah 24:1-4, 19-21.

- It will be a time of punishment - Isaiah 24:20, 21.

THE PURPOSE OF THE GREAT TRIBULATION:

- Lack of the knowledge of the Scriptures makes people think that God cannot get angry against sin and sinners [2 Chronicles 28:10, 11; Job 21:14-20, 30; Psalms 106:21-29; 90:7-12; Isaiah 3:6-11; Nahum 1:2-8; Luke 3:7; Romans 2:3-9; Hebrews 2:3; 10:30, 31; 12:29; 5:24; Romans 8:1, 33-34; 1 Thessalonians 5:9].

The Purposes of great tribulation are:

- The vengeance of God - Deuteronomy 32:35; Romans 12:19.

- To prepare the nation Israel for her Messiah Christ - Deuteronomy 4:30, 31; Jeremiah 30:7; Ezekiel 20:37, 38; Daniel 12:1; Zechariah 13:8, 9.

- To pour out judgment on sinful men in all nations Revelation 3:10; Isaiah 26:20, 21; Jeremiah 25:30-33; 2 Thessalonians 2:8-12; Revelation 6:12-17; 16:8, 9.

- The nature of God and the Word of God will punish sinners who refuse to repent because His unchanging Word declares so and Scriptures cannot be broken (Revelation 15:3, 4; Matthew 5:18).

THE SOURCE OF THE GREAT TRIBULATION

- God is the source of the great tribulation because His wrath and judgment will fall upon the earth.

- Those who refuse to accept salvation must be forced to accept the wrath of the Lord (Isaiah 24:1; 26:21; Joel 1:15; Zephaniah 1:18; Revelation 6:16-17; 11:18; 14:7-8, 19; 15:4, 7; 16:1, 7, 19).

- The tribulation period will be a terrible time as God's wrath will be poured out against all evil and evil doers - Revelation 6:15, 17; 16:5-6.

- In addition, the devil and the Antichrist will release their wraths against sinners on earth. The devil comes down, having great wrath against all that is good and all inhabitants of the earth - Revelation 12:9, 12.

HOW LONG WILL GREAT TRIBULATION LAST?

(Daniel 9:24-27; 2 Thessalonians 2:1-12; Matthew 24:15-22; Mark 13:14-20; Revelation 11:2, 3; 12:6, 14; 13:5)

- Great tribulation will last for 7 years which is called Daniel's seventeenth week. The world has spent the sixth week of the history and the only thing delaying the last seventh week is the rapture.

- In Daniel's prophesy, a week means seven, referring to seven years (Daniel 9:27). The last half of the week, that is the last half of the seven years, 3 1/2 years or 42 months or 1260 days, will be very disastrous because of the wrath of the Antichrist who will break his agreement with Israel in the midst of the week (Daniel 9:27).

CHAPTER 24

EXPOSING ANTICHRIST, THE BEAST?

- John spoke of Antichrist in his epistle to believers 1 John 2:18.

- Even in the Old Testament, it was common knowledge from the Old Testament that Antichrist shall come. Daniel 7:8, 25; 8:23-25; 9:26, 27; 11:36-45; John 5:43; 2 Thessalonians 2:1-10.

- Antichrist is anti-God, working against God's plan. In times of his reign on earth, during the great tribulation, he will fight against the truth; blaspheme God and war against the saints of the tribulation period. This diabolical personality will blaspheme the name of God relentlessly and continuously and literally, will cause millions of tribulation saints to die violent and painful deaths Revelation 13:7, 15; 6:3-8; 8:8-11; 11:3-6, 13, 18.

ADVICE TO TRIBULATION SAINTS

(Revelation 13:9, 10; 3:6; Isaiah 33:1; Matthew 26:51, 52;
Revelation 14:12)

- Whatever a man sows, he will reap, and those who live by the sword will die by sword. Judgment must definitely come on all the evil doers. God's counsel for the tribulation saints is patience and faithfulness throughout the period.

ANTICHRIST, THE KING OF FIERCE COUNTENANCE

— (DANIEL 8:23-27).

- The scriptures exposed the works of Antichrist as an individual who will appear in the end time as the head of the Gentile power in their ten-kingdom federation.

His personality and works are presented in the following scriptures: Ezekiel 28:1-10; Daniel 7:7-8, 20-26; 8:23-25; 9:26-27; 11:36-45; 2 Thessalonians2:3-10; Revelation 13:1-10; 17:8-14.

Antichrist is called with these names and titles:

- The little horn - Daniel 7:8.

- The king of fierce countenance - Daniel 8:21.

- The prince that shall come - Daniel 9:26.

- The desolator - Daniel 9:27.

- The vile person - Daniel 11:21

- The willful king - Daniel 11:36.

- The man of sin - Daniel 2; Thessalonians 2:3.

- The son of perdition - 2 Thessalonians 2:3.

- The lawless one - 2 Thessalonians 2:8.

- The Antichrist - 1 John 2:22.

REVELATIONAL FACTS CONCERNING ANTICHRIST'S ACTIVITIES

- The Antichrist will be strong, vehement, a great intimidator, persecutor, and a demonic genius.

- He will be mighty but not by his own power because he will be energized by Satan.

- There will be a holocaust of devastation that is beyond description - Daniel 8:23-25.

- His cunning is linked to deceit by treachery, by which he will accomplish his purpose.

- Antichrist will be deceitful, treacherous, demonically wise, brilliant, a satanically indwelt genius human personality, and will gain control by lies and deceit.

- The world will wonder at the power of his destruction- Revelation 13:11-17.

- He will appear on the stage in the last days of Israel's history - Daniel 8:23.

WHO IS HINDERING HIM?

- He will not fully manifest until the day of the Lord has begun - 2 Thessalonians 2:2.

- His appearance is being delayed by the restrainer - 2 Thessalonians 2:6, 7.

- His manifestation will be preceded by a departure from the faith or the rapture - 2 Thessalonians 2:3, 1.

- He is a worldwide leader since he comes out from the sea - Revelation13:1; 17:15. Sea represents the Gentile nations, so he must be of Gentile origin.

- He rises from the heathen nation, an empire, since he is a ruler of the people who destroyed Jerusalem - Daniel 9:26.

- Antichrist is the head of the last form of Gentile world dominion, for he is like a Leopard, a bear, and a lion - Revelation 13:11; Daniel 7:7-8, 20, 24; 17:9-11.

- Being a political leader, the seven heads and ten horns are federated under his authority - Revelation 13:1; 17:12.

- He will have worldwide influence because he will rule the world and his influence will come through the alliance which he gained by cooperating with many nations - Daniel 8:24; Revelation 17:12.

- Three main nations and their leaders that will oppose him at his rise to power will be eliminated. One of the kingdoms over which he will exercise authority will be revived or healed - Daniel 7:8, 24; Revelation 17:10; 13:3.

- In order to win many in many nations and rise to power and prominence, he will come up with a peace program to deceive many - Daniel 8:25.

- His personality will be marked by his subtlety, craft, and intelligent persuasions to many for evil, so that as you yield, you will not have anybody to blame - Daniel 7:8, 20; 8:23; Ezekiel 28:6; Revelation 17:13.

- As he deceived the world into covenants and rules them in his federation with absolute authority, he will rule them according to his will. He will change law and customs to suit him - Daniel 11:36; 7:25.

- His major interest is might and power - Daniel 11:38.

- As the head or leaders of federated empire, he entered into a seven-year covenant with Israel, which will be broken after three- and one-half years - Daniel 9:27.

- He will promote idolatrous worships, assume the position of gods, and will receive worships - Daniel 9:27; 11:36-37; 2 Thessalonians 2:4; Revelation 13:5.

- As he promotes himself as a deity, he begins to blaspheme God - Ezekiel 28:2; Daniel 7:25; Revelation 13:1, 5-6.

- He will be empowered by Satan, acts in the authority of Satan who will fully begin to control him with his pride - Ezekiel 28:2; Daniel 8:25.

- Satan will control him and use him to bring lawless system on earth. He will also be performing fake miracles and lying wonders through satanic powers - 2 Thessalonians 2:9-19; Psalm 74:1-11.

- Because of the blindness of the deceived ones, he will rule as if he is God - 2 Thessalonians 2:11.

- He will turn against the children of Israel as a worse adversary ever - Daniel 7:21, 25; 8:24; Revelation 13:7.

- An alliance will come against him and contest his authority - Ezekiel 28:7; Daniel 11:40, 42.

- The conflict will lead him to gain control over Palestine and adjacent boundaries and he will make Jerusalem his headquarters - Daniel 11:42.

- He will be elevated through the instrumentality of the harlot, the corrupt religious system that may seek to dominate him - Revelation 17:3.

- This corrupt system will be destroyed by the antichrist to enable him rule without hindrance - Revelation 17:16, 17.

- This will promote him to double his adversary against the Prince of Princes, His program and His people - Daniel 8:25; 2 Thessalonians 2:4; Revelation 17:14.

- His power, reign, and every activity are only confined to the last three and half years of the tribulation period - Daniel 7:25; 9:27; 11:36; Revelation 13:5.

- His leadership will be terminated by a direct judgment from God - Ezekiel 28:6; Daniel 7:22, 26; 8:25; 9:27; 11:45; Revelation 19:19-20.

- The termination of his reign will occur as he is energized and engaged in a military campaign in Palestine - Ezekiel 28:8, 9; Revelation 19:19.

- He will be cast into the lake of fire - Revelation 19:19; Ezekiel 28:10.

- Immediately he is judged, the second advent of Christ will take place - 2 Thessalonians 2:8; Daniel 7:22.

- This will give way to the Messianic reign and Christ's authority on earth - Revelation 11:15; Daniel 7:27.

CHAPTER 25

THE SECOND COMING (AVENT) OF CHRIST

— MATTHEW 24:29-35; JUDE 14, 15;
REVELATION 1:7; 19:11-21

■ Prophecy occupies one-fifth of scripture, and the second coming occupies one-third of that one-fifth. Of the 333 prophecies concerning Christ, only 109 of them were fulfilled in His first coming, leaving 224 yet to be fulfilled in His second coming. There are 7, 959 verses in the New Testament, 330 of which refer directly to the second coming. Jesus Christ, personally, refers to His return twenty-one times. Over fifty times, we are exhorted to be ready for the second coming of Jesus Christ.

- **The beginning of sorrow announced:** Matthew 24:4-8; Revelation 6:1-17.

- **Antichrist's covenant with Israel:** Matthew 24:9-26; Daniel 9:27; Revelation 6:1-17.

- At the beginning of the seven years period of the Tribulation, Israel will enjoy peace under the false covenant (Daniel 9:27). In the middle of the evil relationship, the Antichrist will break the covenant (Matthew 24:9; Revelation 12:12-17). The Antichrist, which is also the desolator (Matthew 24:16-20), will be stopped by the second advent of Christ (Matthew 24:27-30).

THE BATTLE OF ARMAGEDDON

Immediately after the tribulation, Israel who were scattered will be gathered by special angelic ministry, the elect of Matthew 24:31 are referred to as Israel (Daniel 7:18-22, 27). The second coming will be glorious, wonderful, majestic, regal, and visible (Revelation 19:11-13; Zechariah 14:1-9; Isaiah 63:1-6; 64:1, 2; Matthew 24:29, 30).

- At His first coming, He came like a baby, born by a woman, in humility to suffer, be insulted, to die and save the world, but.

- At Christ's second coming, He will come in full power to conquer, judge, and reign.

- He is coming as a warrior, faithful, true, chief justice and king of the world (Acts 17:31).

THE REIGN OF CHRIST AS WARRIOR AND CONQUEROR

(Revelation 19:14; Matthew 24:29-31; Jude 14, 15; Colossians 3:4)

- Christ is coming to reign as a conqueror with angels and saints appearing with Him. Every raptured saint as warriors shall follow Him, putting on fine linens, clean and white, sitting upon white horses - Revelation 19:14; 2 Kings 2:11; 6:13-17.

THE DEVASTATION BY THE CONQUEROR

(Revelation 19:15, 16; Isaiah 11:4; Joel 3:13-16; Psalms 2:9)

Jesus will appear as KING of KINGS, AND LORD OF LORDS with divine majesty.

- He is coming to rule and reign forever and ever.

- He is coming with all power and glory to reign and rule the earth as King of kings and Lord of lords - Revelation 19:15-21; 20:1-4; Ezekiel 39:17-22.

- In the battle of Armageddon, there will be a great and terrible slaughter on that day.

- Satan and all sinners that will oppose Him will be destroyed by His mighty power - Revelation 14:19, 20; 17:14; 19:11-21; Isaiah 13:9; 29:57; 24:20.

- The Antichrist will gather all sinners as his army from all nations of the earth to fight through the efforts of the evil spirits with his false prophets - Revelation 16:12-14.

- This will be the last effort Satan will make to keep power, but he will fail woefully with the deceived world power he kept in sin under him.

CHAPTER 26

THE RESURRECTION TO LIFE OR THE FIRST RESSURRECTION

FACTS ABOUT RESURRECTION

(Hebrews 11:17, 18; Job 19:25-27; Psalms 49:15; Daniel 12:2; Isaiah 25:8; 26:19; John 5:25, 28-29; John 11:23-25; Acts 24:15)

- Both Old Testament and New Testament reveal the facts of the resurrection.

- Between death and resurrection, sinners' souls were in Hell with consciousness.

- They can see, hear, feel, and the same is applicable to a child of God who dies and goes to heaven (Luke 23:39-43; Acts 7:54-60; 2 Corinthians 5:1-8; Philippians 1:21-23; Luke 16:19-31).

When the time for resurrection comes, physical bodies are resurrected and souls from Heaven for the children of God; souls from Hell for the sinners are united with the resurrection bodies.

- This part of resurrection program is called the resurrection of life, of the just; a better resurrection and the first resurrection.

- It is a separation; a resurrection of a portion of those who are dead, but leaves some dead people, the unjust, in their graves for future resurrection.

EXAMPLES OF RESURRECTION

<u>(1 Corinthians 15:23)</u>

- Christ's resurrection from dead predicted (Matthew 16:21; 17:22-23; 20:17-19; Mark 8:31; 10:32-34; Luke 9:20-22; 18:31-34).

- Christ's body described after resurrection (Luke 24:36-43; 24:31-36; John 20:11-20, 24-34).

- His body was glorified after resurrection (1 Corinthians 15:35-38; 1 John 3:2; Matthew 22:30; 1 Corinthians 15:39-54).

- Our bodies when resurrected like that of Christ will be immortalized, but will possess different degrees of glory.

CHAPTER 27

THE RESURRECTION OF THE UNSAVED DEAD; SECOND OR DAMNATION

MORE FACTS ABOUT RESURRECTION

- Centuries ago, Christ resurrected - 1 Corinthians 15:3-4, 12, 20, 23.

- At rapture, the dead saints will be resurrected - 1 Thessalonians 4:13-16.

- The saints who went through tribulation will be resurrected after 7 years - Revelation 20:3-15.

- At the Second Advent, the Old Testament saints, will be resurrected - Daniel 12:2; Isaiah 26:19.

- All the unsaved dead will be resurrected - Revelation 20:11-15; Job 14:12. This includes those whose bodies were destroyed or devoured by voracious fish into millions of small bits; they will be raised by the power of resurrection - Philippians 3:10; Romans 8:11.

SECOND, DAMNATION, OR RESURRECTION OF THE UNSAVED

(Daniel 12:2; John 5:28-29; Revelation 20:4-5, 11-15)

- Dead sinners of all the ages will also have bodily resurrection.

- At that time, all creatures, including the sea and the graves will give up their dead.

- This part of resurrection program deals with the unsaved.

- People involved in this kind of resurrection will receive eternal judgment from the impartial Righteous Judge.

- This type of resurrection is called the resurrection of the unjust, the unsaved, or the resurrection to shame and everlasting contempt.

- It will take place after the millennium - one thousand years.

- All the resurrected sinners will be punished in the lake of fire because their names are not found in the Book of Life.

CHAPTER 28

THE MILLENNIAL REIGN OF CHRIST

LIFE ON EARTH WITHOUT SATAN

- The millennial kingdom is the coming golden age when Christ rules in power on earth - Revelation 20:1-10.

- It is going to be a reign of Christ for 1000 years on earth.

HOW WILL HIS REIGN BE WITHOUT SATAN'S ACTIVITIES ON EARTH FOR SUCH PERIOD?

- The period will be characterized by peace - Isaiah 2:2-5; 11:1-9; 54:13; Ezekiel 34:25, 28; Hosea 2:18; Micah 4:2-3; Zechariah 9:10.

- It will be a time dominated by happiness - Isaiah 12:1-6.

- It will be a period of time full of long life and divine health - Isaiah 33:24; 65:18-20; Jeremiah 30:17; Ezekiel 34:16.

- The period will be filled with prosperity - Isaiah 35:1-10.

- There will be joy in every labor - Isaiah 65:21-25; 9:3-4.

- The survivors of the great tribulation will be having children but the saints will not - Isaiah 11:6-8; 65:20; 41:8-14; 62:8, 9; Jeremiah 32:27; Ezekiel 34:27.

- It will be a time of theocratic rule, which is a government of the state by the immediate direction of God.

- It will be a rule of God through a divinely chosen representative who speaks and acts for the Almighty as directed by Christ.

- There will be a full manifestation of God's glory through Jesus Christ.

- It will be a time of the manifestation of the glorious universal dominion of Christ's absolute power - Isaiah 9:6; Psalms 45:4; Isaiah11:4; Psalms 72:4; 2:9.

- The judiciary department in which Christ is the spokesman for the Almighty God will be announcing God's will at all time - Isaiah 2:3-4; 33:21-22; Isaiah 42:4; Acts 3:22.

- Christ will seat on the throne as David's son to fulfil the promise to David (2 Samuel 7:12-16; Isaiah 9:6-7; Luke 1:31-33; Matthew 25:21).

- There will be divine mercy, goodness, and divine truth which will be released through Christ the King (Isaiah 40:10-13; 54:710; Jeremiah 33:9; Zechariah 3:10; Isaiah 9:7).

- The reign of Christ will be dominated by holiness - Isaiah 1:26-27; 35:8-9; Ezekiel 43:7-12.

- It will be a reign filled with divine glory - Isaiah 24:23; 4:2; 35:2; 40:5; 60:1-9.

- Comfort will be beyond description - Isaiah 12:1-2; Jeremiah 31:23-25; Zephaniah 3:18-20.

- The millennial kingdom will be a time of justice - Isaiah 9:7; 11:5; 42:1-4; Jeremiah 23:5; 31:23, 29-30.

- The period will be filled with knowledge - Isaiah 11:1-2, 9; 41:19-20; 54:13; Hebrews 2:14.

- Freedom from oppression - Isaiah 14:3-6; 42:6-7; 49:8-9; Zechariah 9:11-12.

- Every curse will be removed - Isaiah 11:6-9; 35:9; 65:25.

- Every deformity will be removed - Isaiah 29:17-19; 35:3-6; 61:1-2; Jeremiah 31:8.

- The conditions that will exist in millennium will be free from social, political, or religious oppression.

- All curses will be removed to give way to abundant life, and the venom and ferocity on animals will be removed.

- Witches, wizards, and evil will be banned, and Christ will minister to every need to give comfort.

- The kingdom on earth will be united; peace will reign and there will be economic prosperity.

ARREST AND CONFINEMENT OF SATAN

[Revelation 20:1-3; 9:1-3; 2 Peter 2:4; Jude 6; Luke 8:28-31; Revelation 12:9; Isaiah 24:21-23]

- Before the start of the millennial kingdom, at the end of great tribulation, an angel will come down from heaven with great chain to bind, imprison, and completely detain the devil in abyss, the bottomless pit.

- He will be imprisoned for 1000 years so that he will not be able to deceive the nations till the end of 1000 years (Revelation 20:3).

CHRISTS REIGN WITH THE SAINTS ON EARTH

[Revelation 20:4-6; Daniel 7:18, 27; Isaiah 32:1-4; Matthew 19:28; 1 Corinthians 6:2; 2 Timothy 2:12; 1 Peter 2:9; Revelation 3:12, 21]

- The saints will sit on the throne with Christ to reign, having the positions and privileges to enjoy.

DELIVERANCE WITHOUT SALVATION

(<u>Revelation 20:7-10</u>).

- God is a just God and nobody can find fault in Him.

- The reason why He does good to all, delivers the oppressed, and helps the helpless is to prove to the world that He is not partial.

- You may be delivered from poverty, suffering, and all physical problems, but if you are not delivered from sin, your deliverance is worse than leprosy, cancer and as good as nothing.

- Punishment, poverty, or prosperity cannot change the devil or the wicked.

- After enjoying from the direct leadership of Christ, full of prosperity, long life, good living, with no disease and war, and abundant provision, people still followed the devil when it was time for good decision.

- Without deliverance from sin, every other deliverance leads to destruction.

- If you are not born again, prosperity alone cannot help you or keep you out of eternal destruction.

- If you are not truly converted, you may pretend to be good when there is no suffering and temptation, but at the moment of decision, you will follow the devil whose nature is in you.

- No matter how much Satan tries, Christ's kingdom is forever and ever.

CHAPTER 29

THE GREAT WHITE THRONE JUDGMENT

THE FINAL JUDGMENT OF THE WICKED

(Revelation 20:11-15; Acts 17:31; Romans 2:12-16)

- This part of judgment is only for the wicked, the unsaved dead, and all sinners who ever lived and died in ungodliness.

- They will be resurrected at the second resurrection after the battle of Gog and Magog at the close of the millennium.

- God Almighty, with great authority and infinite majesty will at this time judge unrepentant sinners.

- This throne, white, symbolizing the absolute spotless holiness of God who judges righteously according to their works.

THE FAITHFUL JUDGE

(Revelation 20:11-12; Deuteronomy 32:4; Psalms 19:9; 33:4; Romans 2:5-16)

- Jesus Christ, the holy, faithful, and all-knowing Omniscient God who is no respecter of persons will be the judge that day.

- His judgment will be final without an appeal (Psalms 9:7; Ecclesiastes 12:14; Daniel 7:9-10; Matthew 7:21-23; 11:20-24; Hebrews 10:28-31; 2 Peter 3:7, 10-14).

- At the judgment day, even the atmospheric heaven will depart, the earth scene of sin will be consumed by fire - 2 Peter 3:10.

THE BOOKS OF RECORD

<u>(Revelation 20:12; Hebrews 4:13; Matthew 12:36; 2 Chronicles 16:9)</u>

- These books contain every evil work everyone has done, every evil deed done, every evil word spoken, every evil intent, or purpose entertained.

- All the unsaved who depend on their works must appear before this judgment seat to be judged according to their works (Luke 10:20; John 5:24; 1 Thessalonians 5:9-11; Romans 8:1, 33-34; Philippians 3:3).

- Those who are saved and their names written in the Book of Life are not going to be involved in this judgment.

THE BOOK OF LIFE

[Revelation 20:12; Exodus 32:33; Revelation 3:5; Malachi 3:16-18].

- No sinner's name will enter into this book, not even by mistake, including backsliders.

- Your name can be in the church committee's book, prayer team, or even among the list of national and international PASTORS, but if it is not in this book, you are finished.

COMPREHENSIVE JUSTICE

(Revelation 20:12-13; Genesis 18:23, 25; Job 4:17; 8:3; 34:10-12; Psalms 44:20-21; 89:14; Jeremiah 17:10; Romans 1:28-32; 2 Timothy 2:19)

- It is wrong to depend on your work or any other work for your salvation rather than the blood of Jesus.

- All evil deeds, everything done since the world began by men in every generation goes into record and will be judged.

THE REALITY OF HELL

- Hell, which is the destination of the souls of people who die in sin of all ages to the time of the White Throne judgment will be emptied and cast into the lake of fire.

- Hell, itself is a place of detention with an unquenchable fire.

- It existed right from the day Satan sinned and got man involved in sin (Jude 6; Deuteronomy 32:22; Psalms 9:17; 86:13; Proverbs 7:24-27; 9:13-18; 15:24; Proverbs 23:14; Isaiah 5:14-16; 14:15; 28:18; 30:33; 33:14).

- Hell, fire is a place of eternal punishment, a fearful reality; an awful state and a tragic fate.

WHAT JESUS SAID ABOUT HELL

- Jesus spoke about the danger of entering into hellfire - Matthew 5:22, 29-30; 10:28; 18:8-9; Mark 9:43-48; Luke 12:5.

- He called hellfire a place of everlasting punishment and an abode of sinners who die unsaved - Luke 16:22-28; Revelation 14:10-11; Matthew 7:15-19; 13:40-42, 50; 22:33.

- The Apostles of Christ accepted it as a doctrine - Romans 2:5-9; 2 Thessalonians 1:8-9; Hebrews 10:26-27; James 3:5-6; 2 Peter 2:4, 9; 3:7; Jude 7, 23.

- At the end of millennium, all those whose names are not written in the Book of Life will be cast spirit, soul, and body into the lake of fire.

WHAT IS THE LAKE OF FIRE?

(Revelation 20:14-15; 20:10; 21:8; Psalms 9:17; Isaiah 66:22-24)

- While hell is the abode of dead souls of all dead sinners; an awaiting trial place of torment; lake of fire is the final eternal home of the devil, his angels, the beast, the false prophets, and all who die without accepting Jesus Christ.

- Second death as we see here is the final, permanent, and eternal separation from God, which is also called spiritual death - Ephesians 2:1, 12.

- Physical death is just the separation of the soul and spirit from the body - James 2:26.

CHAPTER 30

THE NEW HEAVEN AND NEW EARTH

— (REVELATION 22:1-8)

■ Before we talk about the new heaven and the new earth, let us see divine outline for the last days. Days characterized by a denial of God and Christ; denial of true faith, Christian living, sound doctrine, and the imminent sudden return of Christ to rule the world.

DIVINE PROGRAM OUTLINE

- The Rapture of the saints - 1 Thessalonians 4:13-18.

- The great Tribulation - Revelation 6:19.

- The battle of Armageddon - Revelation 19:15-21.

- Satan's imprisonment - Revelation 20:1-3.

- The millennium kingdom - Revelation 20:4-7.

- The great White Throne Judgment - Revelation 20:11-15.

- The new heaven and the new earth - Revelation 21-22.

God in His word has promised to create the new world where the saints will dwell forever. After the millennium, God promised to create an entirely new world that will be free from any taint of sin and evil acts.

SETTING THE PACE FOR THE NEW WORLD

(Revelation 21:1-2; 2 Peter 3:4-7, 10-14; Psalms 102:25-26; Hebrews 1:10-12; Isaiah 65:17; 66:22)

- Because the old earth and the atmospheric heaven have being defiled and contaminated by sin, filled with demonic evil deeds, God decided to destroy them and create new ones - Job 1:7; Isaiah 24:5; John 14:30; Ephesians 2:2.

- This present earth and heaven will be rolled away and burnt up with fire and new ones created - 2 Peter 3:5-7, 10-11.

OPPORTUNITY FOR NEW RELATIONSHIP

(Revelation 21:3-4; 3:12; 2 Corinthians 6:16-18; Isaiah 65:19)

- At that time of this creation, believers will be privileged to enter into permanent relationship with God as sons.

- In the new creation, Christ will comfort, care, and relate with every believer closely.

REWARDS FOR BELIEVERS AND PUNISHMENT TO THE REBELS

<u>(Revelation 21:5-8; 2:7, 11, 17, 26-28; 3:5, 12-13, 21; Galatians 5:19-21)</u>

- God is determined to make everything new, for the new creations - new heaven, new earth, New Jerusalem, new relationship, new inheritance, and new body.

- All things in the new world will be new for new creatures.

THINGS TRUE OVERCOMERS MUST OVERCOME

- The world - 1 John 5:4-5; 2:15-17; John 16:33.

- Sin - 2 Peter 2:19-22; Romans 6:12-16.

- Persecution - Revelation 2:10.

- False prophets - 1 John 4:3-6; Revelation 2:6-7; 15:2.

- Evil Romans - 12:17-21.

- Temptation - Revelation 2:26-28; 3:4-5.

- Satan - 1 John 2:13-14; 5:18; Revelation 12:11.

Deceived people think that to overcome means to succeed at all cost without considering God and His words. To overcome means to prevail, have victory over, and triumph with God on your side - Acts 19:16.

CHAPTER 31

DESCRIPTION AND INHERITANCE IN NEW JERUSALEM

— (REVELATION 21:9-27)

THE DISSOLUTION OF THE PRESENT EARTH AND HEAVEN

(Psalms 102:25-26; Isaiah 51:6; 65:17; Matthew 5:18; 24:35; Mark 13:31; Luke 21:33; 2 Peter 3:7, 10-14; Revelation 21:1; Isaiah 66:22)

- God has decided to do away with everything that Satan and his agents have connection with and replace them with new things.

- This present heaven and earth haven been polluted, defiled with sin, and infested with demons will be burned with fire.

- It is foolishness, ignorance, and myopia to put your trust in the world that is already marked for destruction.

THE GLIMPSE OF THE EVERLASTING CITY

(Revelation 21:9-27)

- This is a glimpse of heaven shown to John in his vision as the curtain was drawn and closed.

- This is a literal heavenly city; a material one and not mystical as some imagine.

- The place is already prepared, waiting for the saints to inhabit as a home - Isaiah 64:4; John 14:1-3; 1 Corinthians 2:9.

- All believers who will keep their faith to the end are already citizens of the heavenly country.

- We are strangers here on earth and ambassadors of heaven - Philippians 3:20-21; 2 Corinthians 5:20.

- Those who refuse to repent and forsake sin will not be allowed to enter the holy new city.

EXCLUSION FROM THE CITY

- The fearful - Revelation 21:8; John 9:18-22; Matthew 10:33-36.

- The unbelieving - John 3:18-20, 36.

- The abominable - Leviticus 18:21-27; Deuteronomy 22:5; Romans 1:18-32; Proverbs 6:16-19.

- The murderers - 1 John 3:15.

- The whoremongers, fornicators, and adulterers - Matthew 5:27-30.

- The sorcerers, witches, and those who use familiar spirits - Deuteronomy 18:9-14; 1 Samuel 28:5-11; 1 Chronicles 10:13-14; Isaiah 8:19.

- The idolaters - Exodus 20:3-5; 1 John 5:21.

- The liars - Revelation 21:27; 22:15.

THE INHABITANTS OF THE CITY

(Revelation 21:2-3, 22-23; 22:3; Hebrews 11:10, 13-16; 12:22-24; Revelation 3:12)

- This is the city that Christ and the victorious saints will be together in eternally.

- It is a literal heavenly city and the capital of the new creation; the dwelling place of the bride, the lamb's wife - Revelation 21:9-10; Hebrews 12:22-23; 11:10.

LIFE IN THE NEW CITY

- Believers are strangers here on earth; our home is in heaven where our father is.

- Our savior is in heaven; our home is there; our name is there, written in the Book of Life.

- Everything concerning us is there; our treasure, life, inheritance, affections, heart, and citizenship are in heaven, not here on earth.

THE LIFESTYLE IN HEAVEN

- It is a life of true fellowship - Revelation 5:12; 19:1; 7:9-12.

- A life of purity - Revelation 21:27.

- A life of perfect rest - Revelation 14:13.

- A life of joy - Revelation 21:4.

- A life of abundance – Revelation 21:6.

- A life of knowledge - 1 Corinthians 13:12.

- A life of glory - 2 Corinthians 4:17; Colossians 3:4; John 17:24.

- A life of service - Revelation 22:3.

- A life of fellowship with God - 1 Corinthians 13:12; 1 John 3:2; Revelation 22:4.

- A life of peace - Isaiah 2:4; 9:4-7; Zechariahs 9:10.

CHAPTER 31

SPECIFICATION OF THE CITY

It will be a disappointment to only hear about this city without entering into it. Hearing about it is not enough; you need to do everything possible to make it into this glorious new city.

NATURE OF THE CITY

(Revelation 21:11-14, 18-21, 23; Hebrews 11:10, 14-16; Isaiah 64:4; Acts 7:55-56; 2 Corinthians 12:24)

- Everything in heaven is transparent; clear as crystal, like unto clear glass, as a transparent glass.

- One important aspect of the city is that it is full of the blazing, brilliant glory of God.

- The gates shall not be shut at all; no night there, no obstruction.

- All the foundation walls of the city are garnished with all manner of precious stones (colored gems).

- The first foundation was Jasper (clear diamond);

- the second, Sapphire (blue);

- the third, Chalcedony (sky-blue agate);

- the fourth, emerald (green);

- the fifth, Sardonyx (red and white);

- the sixth, Sardius (red);

- the seventh, Chrysolite (gold);

- the eight, beryl (sea-green);

- the ninth, topaz (yellow-green);

- the tenth, Chrysoprasus (green);

- the eleventh, Jacinth (violet);

- the twelfth, amethyst (purple).

Because of its transparency, you can see yourself from all points at all times with the fullness of God's glory reflecting from everywhere.

MEASUREMENT AND SIZE OF THE CITY

(Revelation 21:12-17)

The New Jerusalem is big enough to contain billions of people and as many as will find their way through the narrow gate of salvation - John 14:2; Matthew 7:14. The symmetry was perfectly designed everywhere in the city.

There are number of 12s noticeable in the city:

- 12 by 12 gates with 12 angels,

- 12 tribes,

- 12 foundations,

- 12 Apostles,

- 12 pearls,

- 12 thousand furlongs and 12 by 12 cubits!

(Revelation 21:12, 14, 16, 17, 21).

- The city will be a cube, measuring 12000 furlongs (approximately 1500 miles) in length, breadth and height.

- If you take the length and breadth measurements, you will discover that this eternal city will give you 2, 250, 000 square miles in one layer of mansions!

With millions of intersecting layers of avenues in the city, streets will rise up over streets.

HERITAGE RECEIVED FROM GOD

(Revelation 22:1-5; Psalms 46:4; Genesis3:22; Revelation 2:7; 1 John 3:1-2; Revelation 21:23, 25; 22:14)

In the city, there is the river of water of life and the tree of life yielding different types of fruits each month.

- Is there eating and drinking in that city? - John 21:10-14; Genesis 18:6-8, 16-17; 19:1; Luke 22:15-18, 29-30.

There shall be no more curse, hunger, thirst, sickness, or death.

IT IS IMPOSSIBLE TO PROFANE THE CITY

(Revelation 21:27; 20:15; 22:15)

Unrepentant sinners will remain forever outside of the city, separated from God and banished forever to avoid desecrating the city.

CHAPTER 32

URGENT NEED FOR REVIVAL

- Revival is divine visitation to a people, which brings them from a state of spiritual apathy to a renewed and more active attention to holiness and godliness (Jonah 3:4-10; 1 King 18:31-36).

- Revival is a powerful and widespread outpouring of God's Spirit upon people (Joel 2:28).

- It is the visitation of God that changes the moral and spiritual climate of a place (2 King 23:4).

- When revival comes, weak Christians and dormant churches are revived to be vibrant and militant.

WHY DO WE NEED REVIVAL?

- Because many have backslidden and are living a mechanical life without spirituality (Judges 16:20).

- Because of God's anger against sin, wickedness has turned His face away from many (Psalm 74:1-3).

- Because of the reign and prosperity of the wicked against the righteous (Psalm 74:4-8).

- Because of hindrances and delays in the fulfilment of God's promises and evil changes against the righteous (Psalm 74:9, 4-8).

- Because of the increase of many challenges against the righteous (Psalm74:9, 4; Acts 2:4; 4:13-22).

- Lack of brotherly love, increase of hatred, jealousy, division, and prayerlessness in the church (1 Corinthians 3:3-5; Luke 18:11; Samuel 28:6).

- Because of the increase of carnality, love of money, lusts, and covetousness (1 Timothy 4:10; Genesis 13:10, 12-13).

- Because of the worldly influence in the church, fear of the future, and pride (Hosea 7:8-9; 1 Samuel 8:19-20; 2 King 17:15; Matthew 26:70-74; 10:33; Proverbs 16:18).

- Because of the apathy to God's work, God's will, and God's word.

- Because many goes to church but lack Christian experience and true Christ-like life.

- Because many who started in the spirit are walking in the flesh.

- We must react urgently by planning for special prayer conferences, sanctifying prayers, and fasting (Nehemiah 1:4; Psalm 126:5-6; Jeremiah 3:7).

MEANS OF REVIVAL

- Waiting upon the Lord - Isaiah 40:29-31.

- Diligent study of God's word - Joshua 1:8; Acts 6:4; Deuteronomy 8:3; 2 Timothy 2:15.

- Fervent prayers - Acts 13:2-3; Genesis 32:24-26; Romans 15:30-31; 2 Thessalonians 3:1-2; Luke 5:15.

- Renewal programs - Proverbs 27:17; Mark 6:30-32; Matthew 17:19.

- Desire to know God more - Psalms 42:1-2; Philippians 3:10.

- Complete trust in God - Luke 6:45; Psalm 119:60; John 5:30.

- Seriousness in ministry - Acts 2:47; 1 Timothy 4:15-16; Colossians 2:6-7; Ephesians 4:14; Mark 16:15.

PRICE OF REVIVAL

(Ezekiel 22:29-30)

- Denial of self - Matthew 16:24.

- Dedication and renewed consecration - Romans 12:1-2.

- Continuous prayers and necessary confession - Psalm 85:6.

- God is searching for people with vision to revive for His work - Habakkuk 1:7.

BENEFITS OF REVIVAL

- God's consciousness among the people, leading to sinner's convictions, conversions, believers' more thirst for holiness, and fear of God - Jeremiah 9:1.

- It brings unity and divine magnetism - Acts 2:1, 6; Psalm 133; Acts 13:44; Ezekiel 37:1-10. Sinners, backsliders, and weak Christians are drawn back to God and empowered for divine service.

- There will be anointed ministrations that will bring mass conversions, deliverances, and healings.

- There will be supernatural manifestations, signs, and wonders accompanying the preaching and prayers.

- There will be abundant spiritual harvest as sinners of every place, tribe, and religion will be converted - Acts 2:41, 47; 4:5; 6:7.

- There will be abiding fruits of the spirit - Acts 2:42-47.

CHAPTER 33

DEVELOPING SERMON TOPICS

1. Liberation and solemn assembly Genesis 19:12-14.

2. The prosperity of Igbo race Genesis 26:6, 12-33; 28:10-22; 30:27-43.

3. Igbo musts develop their lands Genesis 30:42-43; 31:1-55.

4. Igbo liberation and solemn assembly Genesis 31:43-55; 35:1-6; Leviticus 20:26-27.

5. Ogboni god among the Igbo Genesis 31:19, 29-30, 32, 34.

6. Warning against enemies of Igbo Genesis 31:24, 29-55.

7. The mother of the Igbo. ZIL-PAH Genesis 35:26; 49:19.

8. Why the Igbo are having problems Exodus 1:7-14, 20

9. The burning Igbo nation, not consumed Exodus 3:2

10. Family liberation Exodus 8:22-24; 9:1-6, 7, 20, 21, 26

11. Community liberation Exodus 10:7-11, 21-26.

12. City liberation and solemn assembly Exodus 12:6, 13, 21-23, 26-28.

13. The liberation trumpet for assembling Numbers 10:1-4

14. Liberation and solemn assembly Numbers 21:16, 12-15, 17-20.

15. The Igbo tribe Numbers 26:15-18

16. Women liberation ministry Numbers 26:33-34; 22:1-11; Joshua 17:3-4.

17. Settlement of Igbo tribe outside their promised land Numbers 32:1-15, 16-35; 35:13-15, 1, 2, 29; Deuteronomy 3:8-13, 16, 18-20; 4:41-43.

18. Community liberation Deuteronomy 12:1-3, 8, 9, 12-13.

19. Igbo must be warned Deuteronomy 12:29-32.

20. Igbo must come back to develop their land Joshua 1:12-18.

21. Family liberation call Joshua 2:12-24; Joshua 6:17-18, 22-23, 25; 5:1

22. Tribal liberation Joshua 7:10-15, 16, 24-26.

23. Igbo, return to develop Joshua 22:4,1-3, 5, 6, 7-9.

24.   Warning for Igbo Joshua 22:10.

25.   Present Igbo generation Judges 2:7-23; Judges 3:1-11

26.   Igbo need more than a prophet, they need teachers Judges 6:7-10, 1-6, 11-40. 8:28.

27.   Hatred between Igbo and Niger Deltas Judges 12:1-7

28.   National liberation and solemn assembly 1Kings 18:1-2, 7-8, 15, 16, 17-20, 21-24, 30-39, 41-46.

29.   Partial liberation from idolatry 2 Kings 3:1-3.

30.   Igbo drinks their children's blood 2 Kings 11:1-12, 16, 18, 20, 21.

31.   Ogboni cannot succeed in Igbo land 2 Kings 17:24-41.

32.   Igbo land, civil war, after the war 2 Kings 25:8-30.

33.   Family liberation for leadership 1 Chronicles 28:2-21.

34.   Liberation and covenant to seek the Lord 2 Chronicles 15:3-15.

35.   Church liberation and solemn assembly 2 Chronicles 15:3-19.

36.   General liberation, solemn assembly and feast 2 Chronicles 30:1-10,11-12, 14, 17-21, 27.

37.   Hindrance to Igbo liberation ministers 2 Chronicles 30:1-3.

38. Community liberation and solemn assembly 2 Chronicles 30:10-12, 17-21, 27.

39. City liberation and solemn assembly 2 Chronicles 30:1-3, 13-21, 27.

40. Actions after liberation and solemn assembly 2 Chronicles 31:1-4.

41. General liberation and solemn assembly 2 Chronicles 34:29-33.

42. Yearly program to renew the liberation 2 Chronicles 35:1-4, 15, 19.

43. Igbo refuses to return Ezra 1:1-3, 64; 3:9-13; 4:1.

44. Liberation and solemn assembly Ezra 10:1-19, 44.

45. Liberation and solemn assembly sealed. Nehemiah 9:1-4, 36-38; 10:1-3, 28.

46. Ministers that accept liberation Nehemiah 12:1-9, 22, 24, 26, 27, 43-47; 13:1-3.

47. Call for community liberation Psalm 108:8-13.

48. City liberation and solemn assembly Proverbs 11:10-15

49. National liberation and solemn assembly. Proverbs 14:34.

50. Need for city liberation and solemn assembly Isaiah 1:21-24, 25-27, 28-31.

51. City liberation and solemn assembly Isaiah 24:5-12, 17-23.

52. Community liberation and solemn assembly Ezekiel 14:12-23.

53. Igbo divorced God Hosea 2:6-13.

54. Deliverance through God's people (Igbo) Micah 5:8-15.

55. Liberation and solemn assembly Zephaniah 2:18-20.

56. The spread of Igbo nation abroad Zechariah 1:17.

57. City liberation and solemn assembly Mark 1:33, 32, 34.

SPIRITUAL WARFARE, PRAYER NETWORK

PRAYERS OF DECREES FOR IGBO NATION

Any dragon in Igbo land, I cut off your head. Any evil plantation in Igbo land, be uprooted by fire, in the name of Jesus. Evil rivers from other tribes that is flowing into Igbo land, dry up. Blood of Jesus, flow into the foundation of Igbo land, in the name of Jesus. Lord Jesus, arise and ransom the Igbos wherever they are. Let the redemption power of God fall in Igbo land, in the name of Jesus. Power to prosper; fall upon every Igbo man worldwide, in the name of Jesus.

Let the voice of singing enter and abide in Igbo land forever, in the name of Jesus. Anointing of God, fall upon all Igbo communities forever. Everlasting joy, wherever you are, begin to manifest in Igbo land, in the name of Jesus. Any Igbo person that is born in any part of the world, arise and shine. O Lord, do something in Igbo land that will attract the world, in the name of Jesus. Any Igbo-born that is lying in defeat, arise and shine. Let the yoke of slavery be broken in the life of every Igbo person, in the name of Jesus.

DECREES AGAINST IDOLATRY AND OCCULTISM

O Lord, empower the Igbos to forbid all that You forbade, in the name of Jesus. Any god in Igbo land that has substituted the true God, be exposed and rejected. Any abomination that is going on in Igbo land in form of evil worship, be abandoned, in the name of Jesus. Power to hate idolatry in every form like God hates it, possess Igbo people. Any vanity and foolish action that is being promoted in Igbo land, be destroyed, in the name of Jesus.

Unprofitable worships and defilement of Igbo land, be terminated, in the name of Jesus. Powers that influence people to bow down to images in Igbo land, be cast out. Power that influence people to worship images in Igbo land, be discouraged, in the name of Jesus. Powers of evil sacrifice in Igbo land, be cast out. Power that compels Igbos to worship gods, bow down to images, be cast out, in the name of Jesus.

I withdraw all Igbos from worshipping dead people or setting up idols in their hearts, in the name of Jesus. Any spirit of covetousness and sensuality in Igbo land, be cast out. Any symbol that stands for God in place of gods in Igbo land, be uprooted, in the name of Jesus. Any external or internal idol in Igbo land, be destroyed. Anything in Igbo land that is taking God's place, be wasted, in the name of Jesus.

O Lord, increase Your love in the heart of every Igbo person, in the name of Jesus. Anointing for love of money in Igbo land, break to pieces. Let every obstacle before any Igbo person from serving God be removed, in the name of Jesus. I destroy the anointing of evil entertainment in every Igbo born. O Lord, help every Igbo person to put You first in everything in life, in the name of Jesus.

O Lord, empower the Igbos everywhere to hate and abandon occultism, in the name of Jesus. Lord Jesus, bless and protect every Igbo born that has not joined occult. Any Igbo person that is in any occult, O Lord, help them to come out, in the name of Jesus. Let every occult group on earth avoid every Igbo person. Power to say no to the occult, fall upon every Igbo person, in the name of Jesus.

Father Lord, open the heart of every Igbo person to believe in Your protection, in the name of Jesus. O Lord, help every Igbo born to run to You in time of troubles and not to the occult. Let every Igbo person seek assistance from God and not in occult, in the name of Jesus. Father Lord, help every Igbo person to have full trust in You. O Lord, arise and take away every Igbo person from occult, in the name of Jesus.

Father Lord, close the doors of occultism to Igbo land, in the name of Jesus. Every good door that was closed against the Igbos by the occult, open by force. Let the Igbos become tired of occults, in the name of Jesus. Father, open the eyes of the Igbos to see why they should hate occultism. Blood of Jesus, flow into every occult group in Igbo land, in the name of Jesus. Occultism in Igbo land, go back to where you came from. Any spirit behind occultism in Igbo land, I cast you out, in the name of Jesus.

Blood of Jesus, speak every Igbo person out of occult groups, in the name of Jesus. Any problem in the lives of any Igbo person from the occult, be terminated. Powers of occult groups that are expanding Igbos' problems, be destroyed, in the name of Jesus. Every yoke of backwardness from the occult world, avoid all Igbos. Common problems in the lives of the people that renounce occult, die for the sake of Igbo people, in the name of Jesus. Everlasting God, raise Your hand and judge the occult in Igbo land. Let the presence of occultism in Igbo land disappear forever, in the name of Jesus.

GOD'S PRESENCE IN IGBO LAND

I command the voice of the enemy in Igbo land to be silenced, in the name of Jesus. You, the land of the Igbos, vomit every enemy inside you. O Lord, appear and possess Igbo land completely, in the name of Jesus. Anything in Igbo land that is fighting against divine presence, be destroyed. Almighty God, begin to operate in Igbo land by fire. Every evil covenant that is existing in Igbo land, break, in the name of Jesus. Any curse that is placed upon Igbo land, expire by force, in the name of Jesus.

O Lord, arise and take over every space in Igbo land, in the name of Jesus. Any evil movement in Igbo land, be demobilized. God the Father, God the Son, and God the Holy Ghost, come down in Igbo land, in the name of Jesus. Any evil power that has captured Igbo land, release her. Let the angels that will liberate Igbo land be released by God now, in the name of Jesus. Any evil kingdom in Igbo land, be destroyed. Father Lord, come and rule and reign forever in Igbo land, in the name of Jesus. Any evil leadership in Igbo land, be terminated. Let the foundation of Igbo land drink the blood of Jesus, in the name of Jesus.

O Lord, arise and walk round Igbo land for deliverance. Any power that is fighting against God in Igbo land, be wasted, in the name of Jesus. Any evil leg that is walking in Igbo land in the spirit, break into pieces. Let the liberation power of God dominate Igbo land, in the name of Jesus.

DECREES FOR VICTORY OVER HATRED AGAINST IGBO TRIBE

Almighty God, arise in your power and deliver me from hatred and envy, in the name of Jesus. Heavenly father, command the enemies of Igbo Hebrew nations to make mistakes that will favor us. Every formidable organized enemies of Igbo tribe in Nigeria, scatter and gather no more in shame. Blood of Jesus, flow into the foundation of Nigeria and push away, out of Nigeria every haters of Igbo race, in the name of Jesus.

Any man or woman, anywhere that hates me because of my tribe, you are finished, repent or perish, in the name of Jesus. Any decision taken against me in any place in Nigeria because of my tribe, be reversed. O Lord arise and take the Igbo tribe to her place in life, in or outside Nigeria. Power to recover every good thing the Igbo people has lost in Nigeria and Africa, possess every Igbo person. Any evil hand that will try to write, sign anything against any Igbo person, wither and dry up, in the name of Jesus.

Any attempt in Nigeria, anywhere to destroy the Igbo race, back fire. You the enemies of Igbo tribe, wherever you are, destroy yourselves. Any weapon, prepared or will ever be prepared against any Igbo person, back fire. Every evil mouth, speech ready to speak or deliver against any Igbo person, end to our favor, in the name of Jesus.

Organized evil policy against any Igbo person, turn around and favor the Igbo people in general. Any program going on against any Igbo person in any office in the world, be terminated, in the name of Jesus.

Almighty God, open the eyes of every Igbo person to show them where to cast their nets. Almighty God, bless the work of the hands of every Igbo person in any part of the world. Let the haters and enemies of any Igbo person begin to fight against each other. Every enemy of Igbo person anywhere, especially in Igbo land, be confuse, destroy yourselves, in the name of Jesus.

Any evil brain thinking, will ever think or plan against any Igbo person, receive confusion unto death. Any evil sacrifice ever offered or will ever be offered against any Igbo person or Igbo people in general, back fire. Every enemy of Igbo people in Igbo land, wherever you are, show up and destroy yourselves, in the name of Jesus.

Any government in Nigeria, anywhere that hates the Igbo Hebrew nation, be terminated in shame immediately. Internal and external enemies of Igbo people, on suicide mission, wherever you are, perish alone. Any evil eyes monitoring the activities of Igbo person for attack, be blinded mysteriously. Arrows of destruction, death and violence that will ever be fired at any Igbo person, go back to your sender. Wherever the enemies of Igbo person will call any of us for evil, blood of Jesus, answer for us, in the name of Jesus.

Any evil sacrifice, utterance or thoughts against any Igbo person, expire and back fire, in the name of Jesus Ancient of days, deliver every Igbo person from the bondage of Idolatry and empower us to serve you only, in the name of Jesus.

Let the blood of the Igbo people ever shed in this nation cry against Igbo haters. Every mountain standing against any Igbo person anywhere, be removed by thunder, in the name of Jesus.

1 command the whole creature to rise against every haters of Igbo race anywhere on earth. Anything that must happen for Igbo nation to be liberated, what are you waiting for? Begin to happen, in the name of Jesus.

Every spiritual and physical problem of Igbo tribe, one by one, your time is up, perish immediately. Dangerous and determined unrepentant enemies of Igbo tribe, without delay, fail woefully and perish forever. Every evil altar in Igbo land, against Igbo tribe, be uprooted from your root, in the name of Jesus.

Any evil agreement, conspiracy, gang ups and action against Igbo nation in the past, present and future, back fire, in the name of Jesus. Father Lord, Lord Jesus, Blessed Holy Spirit, arise in your anger and reward every unrepentant haters of Igbo people, in the mighty name of Jesus.

Power to rise above others in my line of profession, possess me by fire. Blood of Jesus, neutralize every evil inherited sacrifice working against my life. Every enemy of Igbo business men and women in any part of the world, be frustrated, in the name of Jesus.

Any roaring Lion in any city of the world against Igbo tribe, be silenced by the Lion of the tribe of Judea. Heavenly father, arise in your power and remove any evil person in authority assigned to fight Igbo people, in the name of Jesus.

DIVINE PEACE IN IGBO LAND

O Lord, by Your power, bring peace in Igbo land as it is in heaven, in the name of Jesus. Let violence no longer be mentioned in Igbo land. Every spirit of violence in Igbo land, be cast out, in the name of Jesus. Prince of peace, come and reign and rule in Igbo land. I command every evil voice in Igbo land to be silenced by the voice of peace, in the name of Jesus. Spirit of wastage and destruction in Igbo land, be cast out. Father Lord, surround the borders of Igbo land with peace, in the name of Jesus. Any spiritual war that is going against Igbo people, stop, in the name of Jesus.

Let the walls of Igbo land be called salvation, in the name of Jesus. Father Lord, make the land of the Igbos a land of peace. Let the gates in Igbo land be filled with praises of God, in the name of Jesus. Any messenger of violence in Igbo land, carry your message to your sender. Any evil sacrifice against the Igbos, expire, in the name of Jesus. Stretch O hand of God, in all Igbo land forever. Let the sun of Igbo land be permanent, in the name of Jesus. O Lord, bring permanent light from heaven into Igbo land. I command every space in Igbo land to be brightened by divine light, in the name of Jesus.

Blessed Holy trinity, come and be the everlasting light in Igbo land, in the name of Jesus. Glory of God, arise and take over the whole Igbo nation. Let the sun of Igbo land refuse to go down forever, in the name of Jesus. You the moon, you must not withdraw your service in Igbo land anytime, Lord Jesus, terminate the reign of darkness in Igbo land forever, in the name of Jesus.

DECREES FOR PERSONAL DISCOVERY

Ancient of days, empower me to discover my destiny and fulfil it, in the name of Jesus. Father Lord, show me my true person and help me to understand myself. Blood of Jesus, speak my destiny out of every evil altar's arrest. Any demonic material covering my original, catch fire and burn to ashes. Lord Jesus, reveal to me why I am here on earth, in the name of Jesus.

Fire of God, burn to ashes every enemy of my true personality. My original, wherever you are now, appear by force, in the name of Jesus.

O Lord, if I am not where I suppose to be, take me to where I suppose to be. Every curse of wrong assumption of who I am, expire. Any evil spirit assigned to misplace me in life; I cast you out, in the mighty name of Jesus.

Father Lord, open my eyes to see my personal true identity. Any satanic door locking me against God's plan, open and release me, in the name of Jesus.

Any power attacking my personal talent, be disengaged and frustrated. Any evil spirit destroying me from my root, I cast you out. Blood of Jesus, flow into my life and release me from captivity, In the name of Jesus.

Angels of the living God, walk me out from wrong place, in the name of Jesus. Any evil sacrifice, offered to take me away from God's plan, expire. O Lord, arise and deliver me from every confusion. I break and loose myself from every unprofitable covenant. Any witch or wizard, attacking my destiny, be frustrated. Any inherited problem assigned to take me away from God's plan, fail woefully. Any evil personality collecting my blessings spiritually, be disgraced, in the name of Jesus.

I break and loose myself from satanic plans and purpose. I stand against every destiny killer assigned to kill me. Every mistake assigned to take me away from my place; I reject you, in the name of Jesus.

O Lord, lead me to the steps that will help me discover myself. Any power contending against my manifestation, disappear forever. I cancel the effect of negative dedication working against my destiny. O Lord, I bring myself back to you for complete deliverance, in the name of Jesus.

You my glory, wherever you are, appear by force, in the name of Jesus. I frustrate every satanic decision against my destiny. Any evil roadblock mounted against my destiny, be dismantled. Every satanic network diverting my glory, scatter, in the name of Jesus.

OPEN DOORS IN IGBO LAND

O hand of God, arise and open the gates leading to Igbo land, in the name of Jesus. Any wall of Jericho that is blocking the Igbos, collapse. Any evil personality assigned to close good doors against the Igbos, be frustrated, in the name of Jesus. Ancient of days, open every gate the enemy has closed against the Igbos. I remove every satanic blockage against the Igbos, in the name of Jesus. Any evil roadblock against the Igbos, be dismantled. Father Lord, open all everlasting gates against the Igbos, in the name of Jesus.

Lord Jesus, command the roads leading to Igbo land to open, in the name of Jesus. Any satanic security officer that is blocking Igbo roads, be cast out. Every good thing that is blocked from entering Igbo lands, enter now, in the name of Jesus. Any evil head that is blocking Igbo gates, be lifted by force. Let all gates leading to Igbo land open and remain open, in the name of Jesus. Let every spiritual and physical door that is closed to Igbos' development open, Lord Jesus, enter into Igbo land and bring every good thing into it, in the name of Jesus.

Doors into Igbo land, closed by idolatry, open by force, in the name of Jesus. Blood of Jesus, speak every gate closed against the Igbos to open. Every demonic conspiracy against the gates into Igbo land, scatter, in the name of Jesus. Let the power of

God appear at every gate in Igbo land. Any door that is closed against Igbos by our ancestors, be opened, in the name of Jesus. I break the backbone of every enemy of development in Igbo land, Forces of darkness against industrialization in Igbo land, scatter, in the name of Jesus. King of glory, enter into the land of the Igbos with heavenly armies, in the name of Jesus.

DECREES FOR SKILL DEVELOPMENT

I command every hidden skill in my life to manifest, in the name of Jesus. Let all adversaries of God skill in my life be put to shame. Almighty God, develop every good thing in my life. Every underdeveloped area of my life, receive divine touch. Every enemy of God's gift in my life, be exposed and disgraced. Any curse wasting God's skill in my life, expire, in the name of Jesus.

Any evil character destroying divine skill in my life, abandon my life, in the name of Jesus. O Lord, help me to meet people that will help me to develop my skill. Any messenger of the devil frustrating my skill, I reject you. Fire of God, burn to ashes every enemy of God's skill in my life. Father Lord, take me to where my skill will develop with speed. O Lord, deliver me from bad company and kill my destroyers, in the name of Jesus.

Power to meet people that will help me develop my skills, possess me, in the name of Jesus. O Lord, give me opportunities that will help me develop my skills. O Lord, increase your presence in my life for skill development. Anointing for creativity, possess me by force. O Lord, empower me to use my skill to please you every day. Blood of Jesus, flow into my foundation and develop my skill, in the name of Jesus.

O Lord, anoint me for global new breakthrough skills. Anything in me militating against my skill developments, I bind and cast you out. Father Lord, develop your skill in me for global recognition, in the name of Jesus.

Every enemy of my skill development, be exposed and disgraced. I command every unclean spirit attacking my development to be cast out, in the name of Jesus.

Any problem in my life hindering my skill development, perish forever. O Lord, abort everything attacking the development of my skill, in the name of Jesus, in the name of Jesus.

O hand of God, take me to my place in life where my skill will be developed, in the name of Jesus. O Lord, upgrade my brain for skill development, in the mighty name of Jesus.

DECREES AGAINST COASTAL POWERS

Any satanic bungalow in Igbo land, be destroyed, in the name of Jesus. Angels of the living God, chase away every evil spirit in Igbo land. Let the land of the Igbos be too hot for all fallen angels, in the name of Jesus. You, fallen angels in Igbo land, I cast you out by force. Any person in Igbo land that is possessed by coastal powers, be delivered, in the name of Jesus. Father Lord, dispossess the land of the Igbos from evil forces. Fire of God, quench every strange fire that is burning in Igbo land, in the name of Jesus. Blood of Jesus, close every evil mouth in Igbo land, forever, in the name of Jesus. Any evil throne in Igbo land, be dethroned, in the name of Jesus.

Heavenly Father, arise and shine forever in Igbo land, in the name of Jesus. Every evil resident authority in Igbo land, be expelled by force. Let the strongholds of the coastal powers in Igbo land collapse, in the name of Jesus. Powers of darkness that is controlling Igbo people, be disorganized. Any weapon of evil forces in Igbo land, be roasted by fire, in the name of Jesus. Lord Jesus, disengage every evil force in Igbo land. Every throne of darkness in Igbo land, be dethroned by force, in the name of Jesus. Father Lord, establish Your throne forever in Igbo land, Let the gods in Igbo land begin to face rejection, in the name of Jesus. Anything that is holding back evil forces in Igbo land, catch fire. Let the backbone of the devil in Igbo land be broken,

You, coastal powers in Igbo land, wherever you are, disappear, in the name of Jesus.

DECREES TO DEFEND IGBO TERRITORIES

Every messenger of the devil in my environment, be exposed and disgraced, in the name of Jesus. Any agent of the devil in Biafra land, be exposed and disgraced, in the name of Jesus.

Father Lord, speak peace into the territory of Biafra people. Any enemy approaching Biafra land, receive blindness. O Lord, block every entrance door leading to Biafra land against her enemies. Any spiritual or physical force marching into Biafra land, be destroyed, in the name of Jesus.

Heavenly soldiers, defend every space of land in Biafra nation. Any property of Biafra people, receive divine protected. Any evil inversion into Biafra land, be wasted in the border. Almighty God, close the borders into Biafra land against her enemies. I cut off the head of any enemy marching into Biafra land, in the name of Jesus.

Any evil personality anointed to waste in Biafra land, be wasted, in the name of Jesus. Every satanic agent in Biafra land co-operating with her enemies, be frustrated. Angels of the living God, defend the territories of Biafra people. Blood of Jesus, flow round the borders of Biafra people all the time, in the name of Jesus.

Father Lord, build spiritual wall round about every Biafra land. Any evil angel in Biafra land, be paralyzed. Any weapon of destruction coming into Biafra land, destroy her enemies. O Lord, arise and defend Biafra land day and night all the time, in the name of Jesus.

I command every internal enemies of Biafra people to be exposed. Anointing to protect Biafra people in Biafra land, fall upon Biafra people. Let the powers of the enemy become powerless in every Biafra land. O Lord, make me a battle axe against the enemies of Biafra people, in the name of Jesus.

I command the enemies of Biafra people to become powerless, in the name of Jesus. Any satanic charm in Biafra land, be rendered powerless. Every enemy of the Biafra people in the land, air and sea, be paralyzed, in the name of Jesus.

Let the stones of death kill every enemy of Biafra people in the gate. Every approaching enemy of Biafra people, be blinded, in the name of Jesus.

DECREES AGAINST IMPORTED EVIL POWERS

Any invitation that was given to evil spirits in Igbo land, be removed, in the name of Jesus. Any evil covenant that entered through anyone into Igbo land, break, in the name of Jesus. I command every foreign god in Igbo land to leave by force now, Anything in Igbo land that is possessed by imported gods, be delivered now, in the name of Jesus. Let the gods from other lands in Igbo tribe be cast put, I discard every invitation that was given to gods from outside Igbo land, in the name of Jesus.

Let the existence of foreign gods in Igbo land be terminated, in the name of Jesus. Blood of Jesus, speak every imported god in Igbo land out. Fire of God, burn to ashes, every imported god in Igbo land, in the name of Jesus. Imported gods in Igbo land, wherever you are now, begin to leave. Let the powers of every imported god in Igbo land be taken away, in the name of Jesus. You, gods from other tribes and nations in Igbo land, disappear. Imported gods in Igbo land, vomit what you have swallowed, in the name of Jesus.

Any good door that is closed against Igbo people by imported gods, open, in the name of Jesus. Every problem in Igbo land from imported gods, be destroyed. Let the priests of imported gods in Igbo land repent or perish, in the name of Jesus. Any established lifestyle by imported gods, be rejected. Lord Jesus, walk all imported gods out of Igbo land, in the name of Jesus. You, the land of the Igbos, vomit imported gods within your borders. I destroy the dominion of imported gods in Igbo land, in the name of Jesus. Let the wickedness of imported gods in Igbo land be destroyed. Imported gods in Igbo land, wherever you are, pack your loads and go. Let the judgment wind of God blow away every imported god in Igbo land, in the name of Jesus.

DECREES OF DELIVERANCE FROM GLOBAL CONSPIRACY

Almighty God, defend me and my people from every demonic conspiracy, in the name of Jesus. Any foreign power conspiring against Biafra nation, be disgraced. I command the brains of the enemies of Biafra people to be manipulated, in the name of Jesus.

O Lord, cause Biafra enemies to make mistakes that will favor Biafra. Spirit of tragedy, visit the camp of the enemies of Biafra nation, in the name of Jesus.

Any dark agent against Biafra people, be disgraced. Any evil arrow fired against Biafra people by international community, backfire. Father Lord, raise leaders in foreign land to favor Biafra nation. I command the policies of international communities to favor Biafra nation, in the name of Jesus.

Every anti Biafra nation in foreign land, be frustrated. Every satanic embargo placed against Biafra nation, be lifted. Blood of Jesus, prosper your plans for Biafra nation in and out foreign lands. O Lord, raise international leaders to move Biafra nation forward, in the name of Jesus.

God of Abraham, Isaac and Jacob, liberate Biafra nation everywhere, in the name of Jesus. Any evil agreement against Biafra nation, local and international, break. I command all evil spirit, local and international to cooperate with Biafra nation. Let the global conspiracy against Biafra nation perish, in the name of Jesus.

Any power of darkness influencing international communities against Biafra nation, I cast you out. Any evil personality in any global office working against Biafra nation, be frustrated. Father Lord, deliver Biafra nation from the conspiracy of international community, in the name of Jesus.

Any satanic pregnancy conceived against Biafra nation, be aborted. Any evil meeting that will be convened against Biafra nation, scatter. Father Lord, deliver Biafra nation from the altars of global conspiracy, in the name of Jesus.

O Lord, raise people in every leadership office to favor Biafra nation, in the name of Jesus. I command any evil voice against Biafra people worldwide to be silenced, in the name of Jesus.

DECREES TO MAKE IGBO LAND THE MARKET HOB OF AFRICA

Everlasting God, make Igbo land the home of business in Africa, in the name of Jesus. Almighty God, empower every Igbo person to cooperate with You. Blood of Jesus, arise and prosper every business in Igbo land to Your glory. Every bad business in Igbo land, be rejected by force, in the name of Jesus. Powers that destroy businesses in other lands, you will not do so in Igbo land. Heavenly Father, make Igbo land the canter of businesses in Africa, in the name of Jesus. I command the world buyers to come to Igbo land to buy. Any spirit that is opposing businesses In Igbo land, wherever you are, be wasted, in the name of Jesus.

Any strange fire that is burning up businesses in Igbo land, quench by force, in the name of Jesus. Let everything in Igbo land magnetize great business, I open every road in Igbo land to accept good business, in the name of Jesus. Spirit of the living God, prosper every good business in Igbo land, I cast out demons that are attacking businesses in Igbo land, in the name of Jesus. Let every good business done in Igbo land be overtaken by God's blessing. O Lord, remove every curse that Is attacking businesses in Igbo land, in the name of Jesus.

Any good thing that will be planted in Igbo land, be multiplied in millions, in the name of Jesus. Let the health of all the people in Igbo land be blessed forever. O Lord, fill the baskets of every business people in Igbo land. Let everything that is done in Igbo land bear fruits in millions. Father Lord, increase businesses that are going on in Igbo land. Every business that will be brought into Igbo land must prosper, in the name of Jesus. O Lord, open the heavens of businesses in Igbo land, You, the land of the Igbos, cooperate with every good business, in the name of Jesus.

DECREES FOR GOD'S ANSWER TO CRYING BLOOD

Blood of Jesus, invoke every blood of the Igbo Hebrew nation ever shed anywhere in the world, in the name of Jesus. I invoke the crying blood of the slaughtered Biafra children. Let the crying blood of innocent Biafra children receive justice. You the Biafra blood of helpless innocent children, cry for vengeance. You the blood of defenseless Biafra women, cry for vengeance, in the name of Jesus, in the name of Jesus.

You the blood of defenseless innocent Biafra slaughtered in the churches, cry for vengeance. You the blood of defenseless innocent Biafra children murdered under labor, cry for vengeance, in the name of Jesus.

You the blood of Biafra children murdered in hospitals, cry for vengeance, in the name of Jesus. You the blood of Biafra women massacred under labor, cry for vengeance. You the blood of Biafra people killed and raped unto death, cry for vengeance. You the blood of Biafra people plundered and killed, cry for vengeance. You the blood of Biafra people looted and killed, cry for vengeance. You the blood of Biafra children assaulted and burnt to death, cry for vengeance, in the name of Jesus.

You the blood of Biafra children burnt to death in their homes, cry for vengeance. You the blood of Biafra soldiers killed ruthlessly, cry for vengeance, in the name of Jesus.

You the blood of Biafra soldiers, kidnapped and tortured unto death, cry for vengeance. You the blood of Biafra children that met their untimely death, cry for vengeance. You the blood of Biafra children that met cruel deaths, cry for vengeance, in the name of Jesus, in the mighty name of Jesus.

PRAYERS OF DECREES FOR IGBO LAND

— (LAMENTATION 5:1-22)

I decree against satanic arrests in Igbo land, spiritual pollutions and contaminations, in the name of Jesus. Father Lord, brush, scrub and cleanse every dirt in the spiritual foundation of Igbo land. Let the fire of God burn everything representing Igbo people in demonic world. Let rusted pipes and holes in Igbo land be washed by the blood of Jesus. I renew the strength of Igbo nation, in the name of Jesus. Let the revelation vision of Christ, knowledge and wisdom of God spread everywhere in Igbo land.

Holy Spirit, liberate every Igbo person to pray for our challenges instead of just talking about them. Break spiritual padlocks and demonic chains locking us in bondage. Remove spiritual deafness, blindness and anoint every organ in the body of the Igbos to function effectively from now. Lord Jesus, break our pride to pieces. Melt satanic deposits and upgrade our brains for scientific exploits, in the name of Jesus. Let the power of God uncover darkness, evil secrets and confusion that are assigned to destroy Igbo people.

Lord, heal the land of the Igbos. Flush out every unprofitable stranger, destroy imported gods and cast them out together with the coastal powers of Igbo land, in the name of Jesus. I command the enemies of Christ in Igbo land to be disgraced, paralyzed, and rendered useless forever. Father Lord, break Igbo nation, melt her, mold her and fill her with Your power. I command every departed glory of Igbo people to come back double, break all our yokes, destroy our backwardness and move us to the top.

Let the spirit of retrogression be cast out from every Igbo person and destroy every evil label in all Igbo lands. Take away the garment of shame, disgrace, reproach, sufferings and give us a change of garment. Let curses, negative words and evil agreements against the Igbos expire, in the name of Jesus. Let the key of prosperity, success and breakthroughs in every aspect of life be released into the hand of the Igbos. Let the hand of God demolish every spiritual and physical structure in Igbo land and stop evil movements in Igbo land.

We close every evil mouth opened against the Igbos. Let the enemies of Igbos everywhere be put in disarray in every part of the world, in the name of Jesus. Let every Igbo-born in any part of the world be favored exceedingly, promoted and preferred above others. Father Lord, remove every full stop, limitations and satanic roadblocks before any Igbo person worldwide. Let the voice of Christ, directions and leadings be followed by every Igbo person worldwide. Almighty God, take the Igbos to their rightful places in life and help every one of us to fulfill our destinies and make heaven at last, in the name of Jesus.

229

rightful places in life and help every one of us to fulfill our destinies and make heaven at last, in the name of Jesus.

DECREES FOR THE DEVELOPMENT OF IGBO LAND

Any evil force, sitting anywhere against the development of Igbo nation, be unseated by fire, in the name of Jesus. Father Lord, thank you for development spirit in eastern land, in the name of Jesus. Any blood pollution in Biafra land, be cleansed by the blood of Jesus. Any curse placed upon Biafra land against development, expire, in the name of Jesus.

I nullify every enchantment made against the development of the Biafra land. Any evil spirit rejecting the development of Biafra land, I bind and cast you out. Lord, arise and dismantle every satanic dustbin in Biafra land. Any evil threat against the development of eastern region, be terminated, in the name of Jesus.

Any god in Biafra land against her development, I cast you out. Every demonic opposition against the development of Biafra land, be frustrated. I cast the spirit behind every problem in Biafra land out by force, in the name of Jesus.

Power to develop Biafra land; possess local and international investors. Any satanic case-file against the development of Biafra land, be closed, in the name of Jesus.

Oppressors of the development of Biafra land, be oppressed unto death, in the name of Jesus. Any serpentine power against the development of Biafra land, I cut you to pieces, in the name of Jesus.

Any evil design against the development of Biafra land, scatter. Blessed Holy Trinity, appear in Biafra land and develop every place. Every enemy of the development of Biafra land, be disgraced. Evil covenants against the development of Biafra land, break, in the mighty name of Jesus.

Envious neighbors against the development of Biafra land, fail woefully. Imported demons against the development of Biafra land, I cast you out, in the name of Jesus.

Any invitation given to the enemy against the development of Biafra land, I cast you out. Any evil hand holding the development of Biafra land, wither, in the mighty name of Jesus.

Any satanic roadblock, built against the development of Biafra land, be dismantled. Any evil wind blowing against the development of Biafra land, be diverted. Any evil prayer and sacrifice against the development of Biafra land, be rejected, in the name of Jesus.

Any evil movement against the development of Biafra land, be demobilized, in the name of Jesus. Any evil program against the development of Biafra land, be terminated, in the name of Jesus.

Any satanic hand writing against the development of Biafra land, be destroyed. Any evil voice speaking against the development of Biafra land, be silenced, in the name of Jesus.

232

232

DANGEROUS DECREES TO PROSPER

By the grace of God, I have travelled and studied history of developed countries widely and my findings are true. Leaders of developed countries are very futuristic while underdeveloped countries chase immediate gains without sacrifice. In the spiritual, there is no difference. There is also a price to pay; a sacrifice for the sake of unborn children. In other to bring the Igbos back to God and into her full destiny, there is a price to pay and sacrifice to make. This time, you have to be involved with whatever you can do.

We need money to sponsor effective prayer teams and intercessors, who are called for such business. We may not get all the results now, but it is an investment for the generation of Igbo unborn children. We must do everything possible to play our part and leave the rest for God. The first part excepted of every Igbo person is to surrender his or her life to God by repenting and accepting Jesus Christ as Lord and the only Savior. Below is one thousand prayer points to be prayed, as we believe God for Igbo restoration and full liberation.

APPRENTICESHIP DECREES TO OBEY THEIR MASTER

Anointing to serve without disobedience, possess me, in the name of Jesus. Let the power of God empower me to be submissive to my seniors. Almighty God, help me to find favor everywhere I go. Any power destroying other apprentice in this place, leave me alone. Blood of Jesus, flow into my life and teach me this business, in the name of Jesus.

Any evil power that followed me to this place, I cast you out. Anointing to submit to leadership, fall upon me now. Any evil power that has vowed to take me back where I came from empty handed, be disgraced, in the mighty name of Jesus.

O Lord, help me to find peace and love with my master. Any agent of the devil assigned to deceive me, be frustrated, in the name of Jesus.

I command the spirit of hatred in people to destroy me to fail. Heavenly father, plant in me the power to obey as I am supposed.

DECREESS AGAINST OCCULTISM

Let all evil plans against God's appointed traditional rulers be frustrated, in the name of Jesus. Let every evil tradition in Igbo land be abolished by our traditional rulers, in the name of Jesus. Blood of Jesus, speak every traditional ruler into true repentance. Anointing to lead every community in Igbo land to God, fall upon our traditional rulers, in the name of Jesus. Any evil throne in any community in Igbo land, be overturned. Enemies of God's appointed rulers in Igbo land, be exposed and disgraced, in the name of Jesus. Any wicked traditional ruler in Igbo land, be removed from your office in shame. Any instrument of failure in any traditional ruler in Igbo land, catch fire, in the name of Jesus.

O Lord, use our traditional rulers to terminate idolatry in Igbo land. Father Lord, use traditional rulers in Igbo land to bring peace, in the name of Jesus. Any traditional ruler that is promoting violence in Igbo land, be dethroned. Father Lord, empower every traditional ruler in Igbo land to live a holy life, in the name of Jesus. O Lord, influence every community member to withdraw their supports from evil rulers. Any evil movement against any community in Igbo land by their leaders, be frustrated, in the name of Jesus. Any community in Igbo land that is under their evil ruler, be delivered. O Lord, raise people in every community in Igbo land to stand against evil, in the name of Jesus.

Let idols in every community be rejected and destroyed openly, in the name of Jesus. Let every activity in Igbo land that does not honor God be terminated, in the name of Jesus. Any abomination that is going on in any town in Igbo land, be terminated, in the name of Jesus. Any satanic agent that is against any good leader in Igbo land, be disorganized. Any evil sacrifice in Igbo land that is crying against any community, be silenced, in the name of Jesus. Let the blood of Jesus flow into the root of every community in Igbo land. Any evil king that is assigned to destroy any community in Igbo land, fail woefully, in the name of Jesus.

Father Lord, frustrate every chief In Igbo land that has vowed to worship idol, in the name of Jesus. Let the council of chiefs in Igbo land stand for the truth forever. Any evil personality that is amongst Igwe's cabinet, be frustrated out of the cabinet, in the name of Jesus. Any witch or wizard that is controlling any leader in Igbo land, be disgraced. O Lord, dethrone any traditional leader in Igbo land that is fighting the truth, in the name of Jesus. Every strange fire that is burning at the helm of Igbo leadership, be quenched. Obala Jesus, speak every wicked leader in Igbo land out of office, in the name of Jesus. Every enemy of the truth in Igbo land, be frustrated and rejected. O Lord, use the leaders in Igbo land to declare the truth. Any wicked leader in Igbo land covering evil in any community, be disgraced, in the name of Jesus.

DECREES TO START YOUR OWN BUSINESS

Every enemy of my settlement and establishment in life, be frustrated, in the name of Jesus. O Lord, provide and touch my master to decide to settle me in peace, in the name of Jesus.

Every enemy of my settlement, be exposed and disgraced. O Lord, arise and help me to be favored by my master. Ability to start my own business, come upon me now. Every satanic delay against my settlement, be destroyed, in the name of Jesus.

Every satanic embargo against my settlement, be lifted. Father Lord, do everything possible for my settlement to be a reality, in the name of Jesus.

Every enemy of my freedom, be frustrated. Blood of Jesus, speak me out of servant hood. Holy Ghost fire, born to ashes every chain of slavery upon my life, in the name of Jesus.

Any evil sacrifice against my settlement, expire. Almighty God, bless my master financially to settle me soonest. You my master, I release you from any evil influence against my settlement, in the name of Jesus.

SPECIAL DECREES AGAINST ENVIOUS ENEMIES

Any evil personality standing on my way to progress, be disgraced in shame, in the name of Jesus. O Lord, arise and help me to maintain what you have given to me. Any man, woman or power envying what I have, be frustrated. Any evil arrow fired at me out of envy, back fire, in the name of Jesus.

O Lord, frustrate every envious people around me. Any evil wish against me from envious people, back fire. Blood of Jesus, speak me out of the captivities of envious people. Any evil gang up against my position, scatter in shame, in the name of Jesus.

Every enemy of my progress, be frustrated. Father Lord, keep me where you have assigned me to operate from. Any evil sacrifice to remove me from my place in life, expire. Father Lord, settle me down and establish me in my Promise Land, in the name of Jesus.

Every enemy of my blessings and progress, be frustrated unto death. Any attack directed against my progress, fail woefully. Wherever they will call my progress for evil purpose, Lord Jesus answer them. Every lie and conspiracy against my position, be exposed and disgraced, in the name of Jesus.

DECREESS FOR IGBO ELDERS

Almighty God, arise in you power and guide Igbo elders aright, in the mighty name of Jesus. Let the gods against the unity of Igbos be frustrated unto death. O Lord, empower Igbo people to love themselves, in the name of Jesus. Every enemy of divine unity among Igbo people, be disgraced. O Lord, raise elders in Igbo land that will stand for the truth to the end, in the name of Jesus. Every enemy of Igbo elder, be removed by force, in the name of Jesus. Blood of Jesus, cover Igbo leaders with great wisdom, in the name of Jesus.

Let every Igbo leader be empowered to prevail over their enemies, in the name of Jesus. Any weapon of mistake that is prepared against Igbo elders, backfire, in the name of Jesus. Let the troublers of Igbo elders be troubled, in the name of Jesus. Any evil force, militating against Igbo elders, scatter in shame, in the name of Jesus. Father Lord, help Igbo elders to take the right decision that will move Igbo nation forward, in the name of Jesus. Blood of Jesus, speak every Igbo elder into right decision, in the mighty name of Jesus.

DECREES TO START AND FINISH WELL

I break and loose myself from the spirit of poor finishing, in the name of Jesus. Everlasting God, empower me to continue every good thing I started to finishing level. You the spirit of poor finishing in my life, I cast you out. Any evil force resident in the land of my program, be cast out, in the name of Jesus.

Every evil sacrifice offered to stop my project, expire. Any evil priest, and enemy working against my finishing well, be frustrated. Every satanic full-stop against my project, disappear by force, in the name of Jesus.

Any strong man standing on my way in life, collapse and perish, in the name of Jesus. Environmental powers, assigned against my project, I cast you out, in the name of Jesus.

Father Lord, increase my faith and will power to start and finish. Every attack against my job because of what I started, stop immediately. Any evil force attacking my finance, scatter in shame, in the name of Jesus.

Father Lord, give me financial explosion. Every evil enquiry in any evil altar to stop my program, fail woefully. Any evil sacrifice offered in my sight or environment, expire and back fire. Heavenly father, cause all the enemies of my projects to make mistakes to my favor. I break and loose myself from the arrest by the spirit of poor finishing, in the name of Jesus.

Anointing to finish every good thing in life the best way and at the right time, possess me, in the name of Jesus.

242

SCHOOL FOR IGBO HEBREW NATION AND PRAYER NETWORK

Anointing to finish every good thing in life the best way and at the right time, possess me, in the name of Jesus.

DECREESS FOR IGBO POLITICIANS

Father Lord, give us leaders with your vision to develop Igbo land, in the name of Jesus. Let the seeds of backwardness in the lives of the Igbo politicians die, in the name of Jesus. O Lord, upgrade the brains of Igbo politicians to achieve greatness. Every weapon of demotions against Igbo politicians, be destroyed, in the name of Jesus. Lord Jesus, bring about political change that will take Igbo politicians to the highest level. Any evil plan against Igbo politicians, backfire, in the name of Jesus. Any evil personality that is working against Igbo politicians, be demoted. O Lord, bring changes wherever Igbo politicians are to promote them. Enemies of Igbo politicians, begin to make mistakes that will promote them, in the name of Jesus.

Father Lord, take Igbo politicians from where they are now to where you want them to be, in the name of Jesus. Any satanic limitation against Igbo politician, be removed, in the name of Jesus. Any witch or wizard that is pursuing Igbo politicians, be exposed and disgraced, Father Lord, take enemies of Igbo politicians out of office, in the name of Jesus. Any evil voice that is raised against Igbo politician, close and die. Let the errors that will promote Igbo politicians take place worldwide, in the name of Jesus.

I cut to pieces every serpent of darkness against Igbo politicians. Let the pit that was dug against Igbo politicians swallow their owners, in the name of Jesus. Blood of Jesus, speak every Igbo politician out of trouble, Lord Jesus, empower Igbo politicians to help themselves, in the name of Jesus. Let the voices of Igbo politicians be heard all over the world, in the name of Jesus. What other politicians cannot do, Oh Lord, help politicians to do them, in the name of Jesus. Father Lord, use Igbo leaders to break record worldwide. Any evil plan against Igbo politicians, backfire by force, in the name of Jesus.

Any death trap against Igbo politicians, backfire. O Lord, help Igbo leaders to lead the world. Opportunity to lead, open for every Igbo leader, in the name of Jesus. You, leaders from Igbo land, begin to lead others with wisdom, in the name of Jesus. Anointing to discover the secret of leadership above others, fall upon the Igbos, in the name of Jesus. Father Lord, command others to accept Igbos for leadership all over the world. Powers that worked with the world's greatest leaders, possess every Igbo leader, Lord Jesus, put Your quality of leadership upon all the Igbos, in the name of Jesus.

Any evil policy against Igbos and their leaders, backfire. O Lord, favor the Igbos and their leaders, backfire, in the name of Jesus. Power to be called into world leadership, fall upon every Igbo leader. Father Lord, help the Igbos to benefit from leaderships all over the world, in the name of Jesus. O Lord, use Igbo leaders to produce good leadership all over the world. Father Lord, deposit Your spirit of leadership into every Igbo person on earth, in the name of Jesus. Any vacant leadership position, be occupied by an Igbo leader, in the name of Jesus.

O Lord, command the world to accept Igbo leaders wherever they are on earth. Let the nations of the earth begin to look up to Igbos for good leadership, in the name of Jesus. Lord Jesus, overpower every enemy of Igbo leadership on earth. Almighty God, deliver Igbo leaders from the spirit of wickedness, in the name of Jesus. Let the backbone of the enemies of Igbo leadership be broken to pieces. Blood of Jesus, take every Igbo leader from problems to the throne. Any Igbo leader, who is under attack, be delivered and promoted, in the name of Jesus. Father Lord, find a way to take Igbo leaders to their rightful places in life. Lord Jesus, vindicate every Igbo leader and promote them, in the name of Jesus.

Wherever any Igbo person is being persecuted, Lord Jesus, deliver them. Let the position that Igbo leaders have lost in life in the nations be recovered. Any incantation against any Igbo leader, backfire. Any evil program against Igbo leaders, end to their promotion. Father Lord, use everything You have created to promote the Igbos. I command all the Igbos to recover all they have lost. Father Lord, empower Igbo leaders to create jobs for the Igbos. Any evil agreement against Igbo leaders, be converted to naught, in the name of Jesus. Blood of Jesus, speak every Igbo leader into positions of authority, in the name of Jesus.

Any evil plot against Igbo leaders, be frustrated. Any evil alliance against Igbo leaders, scatter in shame, in the name of Jesus. Let brains of Igbo leaders overpower their enemies everywhere, in the name of Jesus. Any good door that is closed against Igbo leaders, open by force. O Lord, take every Igbo leader to the next level. Let every Igbo leader get enough support that will promote them above others, in the name of Jesus. You, knowledge and wisdom of Igbo leaders, receive divine advancement. Igbo leaders all over the earth, arise and shine, in the name of Jesus.

DECREES AGAINST OWNERS OF EVIL LOAD

Any evil policy, designed to bring my efforts down, fail woefully, in the name of Jesus. Every evil load that entered into my life by sin, I push you away. Lord Jesus, deliver me from every evil load. Owners of evil loads in my life, appear, carry your load. Any evil hand planting evil load into my life, wither, in the name of Jesus.

Every enemy of my freedom, wherever you are, be disgraced. Every load of sickness and disease in my life, be destroyed by the stripes of Jesus. Any evil attachment in my life, be detached by force, in the name of Jesus.

Any evil program to keep me out of my blessings, be terminated. Blood of Jesus, speak me out of evil carry over. Any evil spirit following me about. Any man or woman, causing trouble in my life, be disgraced, in the name of Jesus.

Every evil load brought into my life by my enemy, drop forever. Any satanic burden in my life, catch fire and burn to ashes. Any evil brain working hard to keep me under any bondage, scatter. Every enemy of my moving forward, wherever you are, be frustrated. Every problem in my life, your time is up, disappear and come back no more, in the name of Jesus

PRAYERS OF DECREES FOR IGBO CIVIL SERVANTS

You, Igbo person in any office, receive the grace to work well. Power to work with joy in the office, possess every Igbo worker. O Lord, help every Igbo worker to do the right thing in every office, in the name of Jesus. Power to work according to the rules, possess every Igbo worker. Every enemy of Igbo worker in any office on earth, be disgraced, in the name of Jesus. Any evil personality that is blocking the promotion of the Igbos, be disgraced. Any trap of death that is set for any Igbo worker, catch your owner. Ability to work in any office, possess every Igbo worker, in the name of Jesus.

O Lord, help every Igbo person to discharge their duties well in their various offices, in the name of Jesus. Any problem the enemy would want to create in any office against any Igbo born shall backfire. Blood of Jesus, speak peace into the lives of the Igbos and their offices, in the name of Jesus. Every negative action taken against any Igbo civil servants in any office, be frustrated. Any evil power that is contending with Igbo workers, be disgraced. O Lord, arise and vindicate Igbo civil servants that are going through persecution. Let the eyes that is monitoring the Igbos in any office be blinded, in the name of Jesus.

Father Lord, deliver any Igbo worker that needs deliverance in the office. Problems that have been designed to frustrate the Igbo worker, backfire, in the name of Jesus. O Lord, arise and take every Igbo worker to the next level, in the name of Jesus. Any strongman in any office that is working against the Igbos, be disgraced, in the name of Jesus. Any determined wicked personality that has vowed to fight the Igbos, fail woefully. Let all satanic agents empowered to frustrate the Igbo workers fail, in the name of Jesus. Every enemy of the Igbos, in and out of the office, receive destruction, in the name of Jesus.

Any power that is attacking the Igbos, attack yourself unto death, in the name of Jesus. Any positional leader that has vowed to remove Igbo workers from office, be frustrated, in the name of Jesus. Any evil movement against the Igbos, be frustrated by God, in the name of Jesus. Father Lord, bring a change that will advance the Igbos everywhere they are, O Lord, make Igbo workers competent managers wherever they are, in the name of Jesus. Any satanic roadblock that is mounted against Igbo workers, be dismantled. Every stronghold of the devil that is standing against Igbo people, I pull you down, in the name of Jesus.

Let all organized evil plans against the Igbos be disorganized. O Lord, bless every effort of the Igbos in every office, in the name of Jesus. Any occult group that is working against the Igbos, scatter in shame. Any man, woman or power that is sitting upon the destiny of Igbo people, be unseated, in the name of Jesus.

DECREES FOR DESTINY RECOVERY

Blood of Jesus, empower me to discover my destiny and fulfil it to the full, in the name of Jesus. Any envious activity that has disorganized me, be terminated. Every arrow of confusion and wrong action ever fired against me, back fire. Any satanic program against my destiny, be terminated, in the mighty name of Jesus.

Forces of darkness after my life, scatter in shame. Any evil personality calling my name for evil, receive brain shock. Any evil power that has re-arranged God's plan for my life, be frustrated, in the name of Jesus.

O Lord, arise and bring me back the way you created me. Any power that has kept me below standard, I cut off your existence. Any evil voice crying against my destiny, be silenced forever. Any power assigned to pollute my destiny, be frustrated without mercy, in the name of Jesus.

Any power presenting me wrongly to my helpers, perish, in the name of Jesus. Any power that has tampered with my destiny, be disgraced. O Lord, bring me back the way you created me from the beginning, in the name of Jesus.

Any family altar, which is working against me, be uprooted. Every evil utterance ever uttered against me by anyone dead or alive, expire. Any power expanding my problem to waste my life, be wasted. Any evil personality that has vowed to kill me, repent or perish. Any occult group that has hijacked my destiny, release it by force, in the name of Jesus.

Every weapon of night raider, back fire. Power that has regulated my destiny out of God's plan, be destroyed. Any power bewitching my destiny, receive destruction, in the name of Jesus.

Anything that must take place for my destiny to function perfectly, take place. Any wicked brain working against my destiny, receive disorder. I pollute the air of my destiny destroyers wherever they go, in the mighty name of Jesus.

Any destiny killer on suicide mission to destroy my destiny, be destroyed alone. Any evil handwriting of envious enemy against me, back fire. I command every creature to work against the enemies of my destiny, in the mighty name of Jesus.

Any power, wasting my efforts in life, be wasted immediately. Every good thing that has left my life, be recovered perfectly. Any stubborn curse in my life, expire forever, in the name of Jesus.

DECREES FOR IGBO BUSINESSMEN

Any spirit of stagnation in the business of every Igbo person, disappear. Father Lord, advance every Igbo business to multinational level. Power to take charge over the economy of the continent, possess every Igbo businessperson, in the name of Jesus. Any satanic policy that is against the business of the Igbos, be frustrated. Blood of Jesus, take the business of every Igbo person to the top, in the name of Jesus. Let the power of prosperity fall upon the businesses of Igbo people. O Lord, empower every Igbo person to be expert in business, in the name of Jesus.

Let investments of Igbo businesses be blessed by You. Lord Jesus, transfer the power of business success into the hands of every Igbo person, in the name of Jesus. Power to grow a business from little to great, possess every Igbo person. O Lord, smoothen the path of every business of the Igbo person, in the name of Jesus. I command businesses of the Igbos to excel above others. Father Lord, catapult every small business done by Igbo person to greatness, in the name of Jesus. Any demon that is opposing the breakthrough of businesses belonging to the Igbos, perish. Let the strongman that is fighting the growth of businesses in Igbo land fall down and perish, in the name of Jesus.

I remove any environmental label attached to any Igbo businessperson. Father Lord, dispatch Your angels in-charge of business to grow the business of Igbo people. O Lord, remove any obstacle that is standing against the promotion of Igbo businesspersons, in the name of Jesus. O Lord, put to flight enemies of the growth of Igbo businesses. Father Lord, release the spirit of business development and prosperity upon the Igbos, in the name of Jesus. I cast out every spirit of backwardness from the business of Igbo persons, in the name of Jesus. Any demonic controversy against the businesses of Igbo persons, die, in the name of Jesus.

Any evil collaborator that is fighting the business of Igbo people, scatter, in the name of Jesus. Any evil personality that is fighting against any Igbo business, receive confusion, in the name of Jesus. O Lord, release the power of number one position to every business done by any Igbo born anywhere on earth. Any evil work upon any business done by Igbo persons, be removed, in the name of Jesus. Let God arise and overpower every enemy of Igbo businessperson, in the name of Jesus. Power for unmerited favor, fall upon any business done by Igbo people. Any strife that is going on against any Igbo businessperson, be terminated, in the name of Jesus.

Anointing for successful business, fall upon businesses done by the Igbos. Every enemy of businesses done by the Igbos worldwide, receive mind blankness, in the name of Jesus. Any demonic padlock that is locking the business of any Igbo person, break to pieces. O Lord, deliver every Igbo trader from business failures, in the name of Jesus. Arrows of loss and memory failure that was fired against any Igbo trader, backfire. Any evil movement, spiritual or physical, against the Igbos, be demobilized, in the name of Jesus.

Any evil character in the life of Igbo businesspersons, be uprooted. I lose every Igbo businessperson from corruption, in the name of Jesus. Any evil utterance that is released against the business of the Igbos, backfire. Any dark kingdom that has arrested the business of Igbo people, release them, in the name of Jesus. Any negative transaction that is designed to destroy the business of Igbo people, be avoided. Any unfriendly assistance to Igbo businesses, be exposed and disgraced, in the name of Jesus. I command every business talent of any Igbo person buried by the enemy to resurrect. Any power that has vowed to hinder the business of any Igbo person, fail woefully, in the name of Jesus.

Let the architect of problems of Igbo people be detected and disgraced. O Lord, release enough health, energy, to every Igbo person for business breakthrough. Any spiritual weakness upon any Igbo businessperson, be terminated, in the name of Jesus. O Lord, defend the business of the Igbos and prosper them, I cast out the spirits of financial failure in the business of Igbo people, O Lord, make the business of Igbo people Your battle axe, in the name of Jesus. Any spiritual and physical wolf that is working against the business of Igbo people, be paralyzed. Let the eagle of Igbo businesses fly, in the name of Jesus.

I command the potentials of Igbo people that was locked up by the enemy to break out. Any satanic prisons that is holding down the business of any Igbo person, open and release them, in the name of Jesus. Any regional altar that is holding down any Igbo business, be destroyed. Any spirit of retrogression formed against any Igbo person's business, be wasted, Father Lord, frustrate any power that is attacking the business of any Igbo person, in the name of Jesus.

DECREES FOR WEEKEND BLESSINGS

Almighty God, arise in your mercy and bless my weekend with all sizes of blessing, in the name of Jesus. Any evil programme against my weekend, be frustrated, in the name of Jesus. Every arrow of sorrow fired into my life this weekend, be converted to joy. You the remaining seconds of this weekend, begin to move me forward. Father Lord, release abundant peace into my life and home this weekend, in the name of Jesus.

Every trouble that has entered into my life this weekend, come out now, in the mighty name of Jesus. You the troublers of my weekend, you are a liar, trouble yourself and perish. Every enemy of my rest this weekend, be exposed and disgraced, in the mighty name of Jesus.

Almighty God, deliver me where I need deliverance this weekend. Any garment of lack and poverty upon my life, be roasted by fire. O Lord, arise and spend the whole weekend with me, in the name of Jesus.

Any agent of the devil assigned to destroy me this weekend, be frustrated. Father Lord, bombard my life with all manner of blessings this weekend. Power to serve God; possess me this weekend and forever, in the name of Jesus.

Lord Jesus, give me enough rest that will carry me through next week. Any problem waiting for me at the end of the week, I reject you; perish. I command all my expectation from God to manifest without delay this weekend, in the name of Jesus.

SCHOOL FOR IGBO HEBREW NATION AND PRAYER NETWORK

DECREES FOR IGBO MINISTERS AND PASTORS

Father Lord, thank You for raising great ministers of the gospel from Igbo land. Any power of sin that is holding down any Igbo minister, be destroyed by force. Almighty God, deliver every Igbo minister from darkness and lack of understanding, in the name of Jesus. Any spirit of fake and deceit in the life of Igbo ministers, be cast out. Every wickedness and manipulative spirit in the life of any Igbo minister, be cast out. Let the root of sin in the life of any Igbo minister be uprooted. I command the power of the flesh, filth and evil to be destroyed in the life of Igbo ministers, in the name of Jesus.

Any evil power or demonic character that is tormenting any Igbo minister, be destroyed. Any internal enemy that is controlling any Igbo minister, be chased out by force. Lord Jesus, deliver every Igbo minister from any manner of corruption, in the name of Jesus. Father Lord, by Your mercy, deliver every Igbo minister from sinful lifestyle. Let the sanctifying power of God sanctify Igbo ministers and keep them pure, in the name of Jesus. Let the power of true love possess every Igbo minister. Let the works of the devil be destroyed in the lives of Igbo ministers, in the name of Jesus.

Let inherited problems by Igbo ministers be destroyed from the roots. Any Igbo minister that is in covenant with the devil, consciously or unconsciously, break. O Lord, arise and take away Igbo ministers from where they are to where they are supposed to be. Let power to overcome the devil and cast out evil spirits possess Igbo ministers now. I destroy and burn to ashes, every counterfeit in the ministry of any Igbo minister. Any evil altar, evil priest and enemies of Igbo ministers, be disgraced, in the name of Jesus. Every enemy of peace, unity and love among Igbo ministers, be frustrated. I close the doors of Igbo ministers to every enemy, in the name of Jesus.

Let any form of carnality, worldliness and witchcraft in the lives and ministries of Igbo ministers be destroyed, in the name of Jesus. Any satanic agent that is assigned to any Igbo minister, be exposed and disgraced. I cast out the spirit of greed, pride, immorality, anger, jealousy, covetousness, love of money, etc., from Igbo ministers, in the name of Jesus. O Lord, by Your mercy, restore every backslidden Igbo minister. O Lord, empower every Igbo minister with Your gifts and grace to work together. Let the power of purity, discernment and discipline possess every Igbo minister, in the name of Jesus.

Lord Jesus, increase the faith of every Igbo minister with the fruits of the spirit. Let the power of the gift of healing and miracles possess every Igbo minister. I command the gift of prophesy, diverse kinds of tongues and interpretation to manifest in Igbo ministries. Let the gate of every Igbo minister open for ministerial breakthrough, in the name of Jesus. Almighty God, direct Igbo ministers and show them where to cast their nets. Lord Jesus, make every impossible thing possible for every Igbo minister, in the name of Jesus.

Let Igbo ministers be promoted and announced all over the world. Power for teaching ministry, possess every Igbo minister, in the name of Jesus. Lord Jesus, raise great men and women of prayers in Igbo land. Let the power of secret prayers, supernatural power and purity, fall upon Igbo ministers. O Lord, make Igbo ministers to be strong in the Lord, in preaching and sound in principles, in the name of Jesus. Let the purpose of Igbo ministers be saintly and spiritual. Father Lord, supply the needs in the ministries of Igbo ministers beyond their expectations, in the name of Jesus.

Let every Igbo minster and their ministry be protected from above. Anointing to reach the top, possess every Igbo minister, in the name of Jesus. Power and grace to fulfil ministry, possess every Igbo minister. Let the great greatness of the almighty fall upon every Igbo minister, in the name of Jesus. Spirit of absolute obedience to the Word of God, fall upon every Igbo minister. Let every Igbo minister be spirit filled and remain spirit filled to the end, in the name of Jesus. Let power to preach to sinners for conviction fall upon every Igbo minister.

Let all the apostolic gifts begin to manifest in the lives of Igbo ministers, in the name of Jesus.

O Lord, arise and favor Igbo ministers worldwide exceedingly. Let Igbo ministers' manifest true faithfulness for service to the end, in the name of Jesus. Fervency in ministry to the end, possess every Igbo minster. Fearlessness in suffering and obstacles in ministry, possess every Igbo minister. O Lord, demonstrate Your power in the ministrations of every Igbo minister. Lord Jesus, give Igbo ministers the vision of open door in ministry. Let every Igbo minister experience increase and multitude followership in ministry, in the name of Jesus.

Let heaven and earthly banks release finances to Igbo ministries. Let problems that defile solutions receive answers in Igbo ministries, in the name of Jesus. Let the voice of the Almighty be heard constantly in every Igbo ministry. Let every Igbo minister be obedient to heavenly visions to the end, in the name of Jesus. Father Lord, empower Igbo ministers to be faithful messengers to the end, Lord Jesus, empower every Igbo minister and give him or her wisdom to evangelize. Let God's boldness, power and humility characterize the ministry of Igbo ministers. Spirit of discipleship and courage, possess every Igbo ministry, in the name of Jesus.

DECREES FOR THE LAST DAY OF THE YEAR

Any evil power assigned to ruin the last day of my life this year, be frustrated, in the name of Jesus. O Lord, arise and finalize every good thing I started this year, in the name of Jesus. You the last day of this year, enter into January to this hour and terminate all my problems. Any evil spirit remaining in any area of my life, I cast you out, in the name of Jesus.

Any satanic hiding place against me this year, receive destruction. You the remaining program of the devil this year, I am not available. Any problem in my life that has vowed to follow me into next year, expire, in the name of Jesus.

Any satanic soldier waiting to attack me in the borders of this year, kill yourself. Every enemy on suicide mission anywhere for my sake, perish alone. Any evil movement anywhere against me this year, be crippled, in the name of Jesus.

Any evil brain thinking against me this year, repent or perish. Anything that must happen for me to end this year according to God's plan, happen now.

DECREESS FOR IGBO SCIENTISTS

Let the spirit of greatness possess Igbo scientists worldwide. Anointing to discover new things that will benefit the world, possess the Igbos, in the name of Jesus. Grace of God to influence civilization in every nation, arrest the Igbos. I command the spirit of impossibility to abandon all the Igbos, in the name of Jesus. Power to locate where mineral resources are in any land, possess Igbo children. Father Lord, deposit scientific power upon every Igbo born, in the name of Jesus. O Lord, use Igbo scientists to discover new things worldwide, in the name of Jesus.

Every enemy of Igbo scientist in the world, be disgraced, O Lord, open every gate closed against science for the Igbos, in the name of Jesus. Let opportunities that will announce all scientists from Igbo land come. O Lord, bless every scientist from Igbo land above others in every nation, in the name of Jesus. Let the spirit of technology possess scientists from Igbo land. O Lord, increase the number of Igbo scientists by Your power, in the name of Jesus. Let men and women with intellectual capital be raised among Igbo people. Let a single scientific discovery by an Igbo person change the economy of the world, in the name of Jesus.

Let the brain of one Igbo scientist overpower the rest from other nations. Power to conquer the world, possess all Igbo scientist, in the name of Jesus. Power to develop the nation's technology, possess Igbo scientists, in the name of Jesus. O Lord, empower Igbo scientists to take over air transportation globally. Any area of science that is yet to be discovered, be discovered by Igbo scientists. O Lord, empower Igbo scientists to take over the seven seas of the world through their discoveries. Ancient of days, bless Igbo scientists with divine knowledge above others. Father Lord, empower Igbo scientists to discover software that will rule the world, in the name of Jesus.

DECREES FOR GODLY CONNECTIONS

Anointing to start meeting the right people in life everywhere I go, possess me, in the name of Jesus. Almighty God, arrange for meetings that will bring me to my godly helpers. Any power bringing wrong people on my way, be frustrated henceforth. Every unfriendly friend already in my life, the door is open, walk out, in the name of Jesus.

Father Lord, lead me to people that matters so much in my life. Any enemy waiting for me anywhere on earth, leave before my arrival. Angels of the living God, take me to where God wants me to be in life, in the mighty name of Jesus.

Almighty God, connect me to the right people in life. Lord Jesus, connect me to businesses that will take me to the next level. Spirit of the living God, guide me to my greatness in life, in the name of Jesus.

O Lord, settle me and establish me in life. I command all my steps to be guided by God from now. Father Lord, deliver me from the camp of my enemies. O Lord, connect me to every good office, thrones and establishments, in the name of Jesus.

Every arrow of confusion and deceit in my life, come out and go back to your sender, in the name of Jesus.

DECREESS FOR IGBO STUDENTS

Lord Jesus, fortify every Igbo student with the right knowledge. I counter every evil movement against any Igbo student worldwide. Any evil power that is assigned to stop any Igbo student, be frustrated, in the name of Jesus. Any satanic blockage against any Igbo student, be removed. Every messenger of failure against Igbo students, carry your message back. Any evil altar that is attacking any Igbo student, scatter by fire, in the name of Jesus. O Lord, assist Igbo students to aspire for first class, Father Lord, empower every Igbo student to be committed for the best, in the name of Jesus.

O Lord, develop the brain of every Igbo student to achieve the best. Let the glory of every Igbo student begin to shine. Power to surpass other students in any school, fall upon every Igbo student. Blood of Jesus, help every Igbo student to outshine every other student, in the name of Jesus. Anointing to be distinguished as the best, catch every student, in the name of Jesus. Let Igbo students be first in their positions at school. Let every teacher see the reason to promote every Igbo student. Let the performance of every Igbo student be outstanding, in the name of Jesus.

Let Igbo students be exceptional and the best of the best. O Lord, upgrade the brain of every Igbo student to perfection, in the name of Jesus. Let every Igbo student aspire for perfect scores in every examination. Let the spirit of brilliance possess every Igbo student. Father Lord, empower Igbo students to be wiser than their teachers. Let the thinking faculties of every Igbo student be perfectly organized, in the name of Jesus. Let the anointing for best understanding fall upon every Igbo student. Father Lord, empower every Igbo student with the best thought energy, in the name of Jesus.

Lord Jesus, upgrade the mental storehouse of every Igbo student. O Lord, give every Igbo student the ability to deal with real facts of life, in the name of Jesus. O Lord, arise and assist every Igbo student in his or her exams. Any Igbo student that is suffering from brain failure, receive divine healing. Any evil altar or priest that is manipulating every Igbo student, be disgraced, in the name of Jesus. Spirit of rising and falling and memory failure, I cast you out of Igbo students. O Lord, perform miracles in the brains of Igbo students, in the name of Jesus. Father Lord, give Igbo student quick solution in every exam. Power of God that helped Daniel to excel, possess every Igbo student, in the name of Jesus.

Any power that is manipulating the brains of Igbo students, be disgraced. Any power that is stealing information from Igbo students, die without mercy, in the name of Jesus. Heavenly Father, release Your power of greatness upon Igbo students. Any witchcraft animal in the brain of any Igbo student, die. Any charm that is attacking the minds of Igbo students, expire, in the name of Jesus. Any curse that is placed upon the academic life of any Igbo student, expire. Any evil sacrifice that is offered against any Igbo student, expire. Any spell, jinx and demonic incantation rendered against any Igbo student, be cancelled. Blood of Jesus, speak every Igbo student out of trouble. Fire of God, burn to ashes every problem in the life of every Igbo student, in the name of Jesus.

Any satanic blockage against the academics of Igbo students, be removed. Father Lord, stock the brains of Igbo students with the right information. Almighty God, empower Igbo students to excel above their equals. O Lord, deliver every Igbo student from evil characters and bad company. Any agent of the devil that is assigned to distract any Igbo student, be disappointed. Any chain of academic failure that is holding down any Igbo student, break. Any satanic padlock in the brain of any Igbo student, break to pieces. O Lord, show Your Almightiness in the lives of all Igbo students, in the name of Jesus.

Any evil altar that is manipulating any Igbo student, scatter. I command any institutional altar that was assigned to frustrate Igbo students to be dismantled. Any evil personality that is working against any Igbo student, be disgraced, in the name of Jesus. Let every evil sacrifice offered against any Igbo student expire. Any spiritual or physical Goliath that is standing against any Igbo student, collapse. Any evil exchange to deny any Igbo student victory, be reversed, in the name of Jesus. Let the presence of God dominate the activities of Igbo students. Any messenger of failure that is empowered to distract Igbo students, take back your message, in the name of Jesus.

DECREES FOR JOURNEY MERCIES

Almighty God, bless every movement I will be involved in this year, in the name of Jesus. Every enemy of this journey, begin to sleep until I reach my destinations. Every weapon of darkness against this journey, backfire, in the name of Jesus.

Every unprofitable movement against this journey, be demobilized. Any evil utterance against this journey, expire. Any evil sacrifice against this journey, be rejected, in the name of Jesus.

O Lord, arise, start and end this journey to the shame of the devil. Angel of God, occupy every space on the air, road, sea and every parts of my journeys in life, in the name of Jesus.

Any spirit of accident and death assigned against my journeys in life, be frustrated. Power to start all my journeys and end well, possess me. Any evil prophecies against my movement in life, expire prematurely, in the name of Jesus.

O Lord, fulfil the purpose of every journey I will embark in life. Every satanic road-block against any of my journeys in life, be removed.

DECREES FOR IGBO YOUTHS

Father Lord, release Your grace to all Igbo youth to abandon their plans that is not Your will. Every organized darkness that is working against Igbo youths, be disorganized, in the name of Jesus. Every arrow of immorality that was fired at Igbo youths, I fire you back, in the name of Jesus. Any power from the satanic kingdom that has vowed to defile Igbo youths, die. Blood of Jesus, flow into the lives of every Igbo youth and cleanse them, in the name of Jesus. Any demonic practice that is devouring Igbo youths, be destroyed. Evil male and female friendships among Igbo youths, be terminated, in the name of Jesus.

Any evil power that was assigned to waste Igbo youths, be wasted. Any spirit of lust, empowered to destroy any Igbo youth, be cast out. The love of money in the life of any Igbo youth, I cast you out. Any demonic courage in the life of any Igbo youth, die, in the name of Jesus. Any spirit of rape that is living inside any Igbo youth, be cast out. I command the spirit of worldliness and carnality in any Igbo youth to disappear. Let every Igbo youth arise and reject carnal limitations and foolishness, in the name of Jesus. Any evil practice and pleasure that is common among youths, Igbo youths are not your candidates. Power to serve the only true God, possess every Igbo youth. O Lord, empower every youth in Igbo land to say 'No' to sin, in the name of Jesus.

Lord Jesus, help every youth from the Igbo land to be truly born-again. Anointing to love God above self, fall upon every Igbo youth, in the name of Jesus. O Lord, help every Igbo youth to hear, read and obey Your Word. Power to be faithful to God until the end, fall upon every Igbo youth, in the name of Jesus. Blood of Jesus, cleanse every Igbo youth from the power of sin. Power of God that came upon Daniel in his youth, possess every Igbo youth, in the name of Jesus. Lord Jesus, give every Igbo youth the power to overcome every stress without sin. Father Lord, help Igbo youths to succeed and serve You in every situation. Blessed Holy Spirit, give every Igbo youth moral strength to succeed, in the name of Jesus.

Courage to face any condition and become better in life, possess every Igbo youth. Father Lord, help every Igbo youth to have full confidence in You. Let the wisdom of Daniel possess every Igbo youth, in the name of Jesus. Let the nine fruits of the spirit possess every Igbo youth, I command Igbo youths to reject evil invitations no matter the gain, in the name of Jesus. Power to obey God's Word and the law of every nation, possess every Igbo youth, Father Lord, help Igbo youths to flee from youthful lust, in the name of Jesus.

O Lord, help Igbo youths to shun violence, O Lord help Igbo youths to defend their faith in Christ even in Babylon. Ancient of days, empower every Igbo youth to be victorious in any battle, in the name of Jesus. O Lord, help every Igbo youth to face any challenge until victory comes. Any demonic character that is common among Igbo youths, your time is up, die. O Lord, help Igbo youths to live transparent lives, in the name of Jesus.

Almighty God, use every Igbo youth to fight insecurity everywhere. O Lord, empower Igbo youths to lift up the banner of the king of kings, in the name of Jesus. Any burning fiery furnace against any Igbo youth, quench by the blood of Jesus. Let every enemy of Igbo youth all over the world be put to shame, in the name of Jesus. Any evil tongue that will rise against Igbo youths be silenced. Arrows of deception, conspiracy, strife and division fired at Igbo youths, backfire. O Lord arise and contend with them that contend with Igbo youths. Any evil agreement among Igbo youths, scatter in shame. Any fire of demonic opposition that is burning against Igbo youths, quench, in the name of Jesus.

O Lord, help Igbo youths to enjoy your presence at all times. Blood of Jesus, help every Igbo youth to walk in Your liberty, in the name of Jesus. Every yoke of oppression, injustice and denial against Igbo youths break. Father Lord, help every Igbo youth to overcome trials and tribulations. O God, arise and trouble the troublers of Igbo youths, in the name of Jesus. Let the promise of God be fulfilled in the lives of Igbo youths. O Lord, raise youths like Daniel, Shedrack, Meshach, and Abednego in Igbo land, in the name of Jesus.

Father Lord, empower Igbo youths to be expert in spiritual battles. Blood of Jesus, put the whole armor of God upon every youth from Igbo land, in the name of Jesus. Any door that was closed by the devil in any nation, open to Igbo youths. O Lord, use Igbo youths to destroy impossibilities in the world. Let the power of divine discretion come upon every Igbo youth. Father Lord, mobilize Igbo youths against the devil in every nation, in the name of Jesus. Let every Igbo youth be empowered by God to discover new things. Let the agenda of the devil be aborted by Igbo youths, worldwide, in the name of Jesus.

Anointing for financial exploits, fall upon every Igbo youth. Let the talent of every youth in Igbo land be discovered early, in the name of Jesus. Almighty God, put Your leadership gifts into the lives of Igbo youths. Let every Igbo youth excel above others in every competition, in the name of Jesus. Blood of Jesus, speak every Igbo youth into greatness. I command every Igbo youth to find their places in life and occupy them, in the name of Jesus. Let the talents of Igbo youths be announced and recognized worldwide. Father Lord, empower every Igbo youth to cut the head of dragons in every nation. Power to create jobs, wealth and industries, fall upon every Igbo youth. O Lord, use every Igbo youth to end the activities of the devil, in the name of Jesus.

DECREES FOR QUICK SALES OF PRODUCTS

Any power holding my product down without sales, I bind and cast you out, in the name of Jesus. Father Lord, command all my customers to appear and buy my goods. I command the demands for the goods in my shop to increase. Every enemy of my buying and selling, wherever you are, be disgraced, in the name of Jesus.

You the spirit that chase away my customers, I break your backbone. Any satanic traffic officer chasing my customers away, collapse and vanish. Let the sword of death cut off the head of the enemies of my business, in the name of Jesus.

Every good I will bring into this shop will receive automatic buyers. O Lord, prosper my buyers to get money to buy all my goods. Anointing to buy and sell according to God's plan, possess me, in the name of Jesus, in the name of Jesus.

Power to receive new customers and maintain old ones, possess me. Any evil sacrifice against my quick sales, expire. Any witch or wizard working against my buying and selling, be frustrated, in the name of Jesus.

O Lord, release men and women that will assist me in buying and selling. Father Lord, bulldoze good buyers into my business. Any evil power attacking the sales of my goods with reasonable prices, I bind and cast you out, in the name of Jesus.

I command all that needs my product to locate me with ease to purchase them without struggle, in the name of Jesus.

DECREESS FOR IGBO APPRENTICE

Anointing for extraordinary skills, possess every Igbo apprentice. Let every Igbo apprentice receive the best experience to excel, in the name of Jesus. I command the spirit of novice to be conquered by every Igbo apprentice, in the name of Jesus. Let every Igbo apprentice be filled with the spirit of wisdom to learn. Let the brains of the entire Igbo apprentice be occupied with divine knowledge, in the name of Jesus. O Lord, empower every Igbo apprentice to discover new business skills. Blood of Jesus, flow into the lives of all Igbo apprentices and prosper them, in the name of Jesus. Power to discover new breakthrough ideas, possess every Igbo apprentice. Let the secrets of prosperity possess every Igbo apprentice, in the name of Jesus.

Let the hearts of Igbo apprentice be filled with wisdom. Father Lord, open the eyes of the entire Igbo apprentices to see You, in the name of Jesus. Any evil power that is attacking Igbo apprentice, be disgraced. Power to serve without complaints, possess every Igbo apprentice. O Lord, help all Igbo apprentice to be truly born-again, in the name of Jesus. Let all Igbo apprentice serve with humility and love. O Lord, give every Igbo apprentice the vision of tomorrow. Power that helped Samuel to serve well, possess every Igbo apprentice, in the name of Jesus.

I break and loose every Igbo apprentice from the yoke of disobedience. Any power that is fighting Igbo apprentices from getting the best knowledge, die, in the name of Jesus. Blood God Jesus, keep every Igbo apprentice until the day of their freedom. Any arrow of defeat fired at Igbo apprentices, backfire. Any temptation before any Igbo apprentice, end to their favor, in the name of Jesus. O Lord, let every Igbo apprentice discover his or her talent while serving. Power that made Jacob to serve Laban faithfully, possess every Igbo apprentice. O Lord, help every Igbo apprentice to live up to his or her master's expectation, in the name of Jesus.

O Lord, better the relationship between the Igbo apprentice and their masters. Father Lord, help all Igbo apprentice to serve with God's fear, in the name of Jesus. Any problem in the lives of Igbo apprentices, receive solution, Ancient of days, help every Igbo apprentice to serve willingly, in the name of Jesus. Let the spirit of gentleness and godliness possess every Igbo apprentice. Holy Ghost fire, burn to ashes every problem of Igbo apprentice, in the name of Jesus. O Lord, help every Igbo apprentice to establish good relationship with his or her master. Let the spirit of hard work possess every Igbo apprentice. O Lord, deliver all Igbo apprentice from hatred and rejections, in the name of Jesus.

Father Lord, help every Igbo apprentice not to overstay at his or her master's place. Let every Igbo apprentice believe in God and have faith in Him. O Lord, let pride be nowhere near any Igbo apprentice, in the name of Jesus. Every adversary of Igbo apprentice, be exposed and be disgraced. Sudden promotion and responsibility will not be seen among Igbo apprentice. O Lord, help every Igbo apprentice to move to the next level after service, in the name of Jesus. O Lord, let every Igbo apprentice be the next in Your list of promotion. O Lord, promote every Igbo apprentice to be settled at the end of his or her service. Power to receive rewards and support after service, possess Igbo apprentice, in the name of Jesus.

O Lord, expose Your master plan to every Igbo apprentice in the day of his freedom. Let the character of every apprentice change for the better, in the name of Jesus. Any evil power that is contending with the faith of every Igbo apprentice, be disgraced. Any Jezebel or Delilah in the life of any Igbo apprentice, be frustrated. O Lord, help every Igbo apprentice to reject invitations to sin, in the name of Jesus. Father Lord, empower every Igbo apprentice to endure to the end. Let every Igbo apprentice overcome every trial and temptation, in the name of Jesus.

Any spiritual warfare going on against any Igbo apprentice, be frustrated. Any power that is assigned to waste the destiny of any Igbo apprentice, die. The power that wastes other apprentice, Igbo apprentices are not your candidates, in the name of Jesus. O Lord, have mercy upon every Igbo apprentice.

Any evil arrow that was fired at any Igbo apprentice, backfire, in the name of Jesus. O Lord, empower every Igbo apprentice to fulfil his or her destiny. Any evil sacrifice that was offered against any Igbo apprentice; expire. Father Lord, speak every Igbo apprentice to great greatness. Heavenly joy, minister to all Igbo apprentice at the end of their services. Any war that is designed to waste any Igbo apprentice, end to their favor. Any evil tongue that is speaking against any Igbo apprentice, be silenced, in the name of Jesus.

DECREES OF PROTECTION FROM THE ENEMY

Almighty God, command your protection to manifest in my life everywhere I go, in the mighty name of Jesus. I command the eyes and the legs of my unrepentant enemies to be blinded and crippled, in the name of Jesus. Father Lord, protect me from the attacks of my enemies. Any enemy walking about to attack me, collapse and expire. Angels of the living God, protect me from every enemy. You my enemies, wherever you are now, repent or perish, in the name of Jesus.

 Any evil hand assigned to destroy me, dry up by fire. Blood of Jesus, silence every weapon of the enemy against my life. Unrepentant enemies from my back, front, ups and down, slump and vanish forever, in the name of Jesus.

Every rope designed by my enemy to reach me, I cut you short. Father Lord, let your protection be all around me, days and nights. You the remaining days of my life on earth, overcome all my enemies, in the mighty name of Jesus.

Every weapon prepared against me by my enemies, be roasted by fire. I command every creature to work against my enemies forever, in the name of Jesus. Angels of the living God, move me and my family to a place of safety in times of troubles, in the name of Jesus. Every enemy of divine peace in my life, fail woefully and be frustrated, in the mighty name of Jesus. Any evil pregnancy conceived against me spiritually or physically, be aborted, in the name of Jesus. Any war going on against my destiny to waste my life, end to my favor, in the name of Jesus. Any mountain standing against my glory and peace, be removed by thunder, in the name of Jesus.

DECREES FOR IGBO MARRIAGES

Blood of Jesus, speak every Igbo family out of trouble. Any sinful lifestyle that is dominating any Igbo family, be destroyed, in the name of Jesus. I cast out every spirit of drunkenness in any Igbo family. O Lord, deliver any Igbo family that is captured by any evil addiction, in the name of Jesus. Father Lord, empower every Igbo family to abstain from any evil, I cast out the spirit of unfaithfulness from every Igbo family. Let the bodies of everyone from Igbo tribe be dedicated to God, in the name of Jesus. Blood of Jesus, flow into the root of every Igbo family. Power to walk in the Spirit, possess every Igbo family, in the name of Jesus.

O Lord, empower every Igbo family to speak the truth boldly always. Let the power of God enter into every Igbo family with singing and praises, Spirit of thanksgiving, possess every Igbo family. Let the fear of God overtake every Igbo family, in the name of Jesus. I command every Igbo family to abort every problem by force. Power to submit to one another in every Igbo family, appear. Anointing to live together in peace in every Igbo family, possess all Igbos, in the name of Jesus. Blood of Jesus, enter into every Igbo family and perfect Your work. Let the spirit to yield and submit to authority possess every Igbo family, in the name of Jesus.

I command every wife in Igbo family to joyfully submit to their husbands. Let every Igbo wife love her husband and submit as unto the Lord, in the name of Jesus. Father Lord, help every Igbo husband to love his wife like his own body. Power to work and provide for the family, possess every Igbo man, in the name of Jesus. O Lord, give every woman that will be married to Igbo man grace to submit. O Lord, raise women like Sarah, Esther, Mary, Shunammite woman, etc., from among Igbo women, in the name of Jesus.

I command the true love to be seen in every Igbo family. O Lord, bring perfect peace and other fruits of the spirit in every Igbo family. O Lord, bless every Igbo marriage with godly children. Let every child born to Igbo parents grow in the fear of God, in the name of Jesus. Blood of Jesus, flow into the foundation of every Igbo child and form their character. I forbid any evil transfer on parents from entering into any Igbo born, in the name of Jesus. I command the spirit of sin to be uprooted from every Igbo child. Lord Jesus, I bring every Igbo child to You for Your blessing. Spirit of obedience, possess every child from Igbo home, in the name of Jesus.

I command every Igbo child to receive good home training and practice it. O Lord, bring divine orderliness into every Igbo family. Father Lord, help every Igbo child to obey the law of God and every nation. Let the blessings of obedience come upon Igbo children, in the name of Jesus. Every punishment that is meant for disobedient children, avoid Igbo children. O Lord, help Igbo children to take their stand to obey God at all cost, like Daniel. Rewards for true obedience, arrest every Igbo child. O Lord, help Igbo parents to be committed to the training of their children, in the name of Jesus.

Father Lord, perfect the relationships of Igbo husbands and their wives. Any evil force that is assigned to destroy any Igbo family, scatter. Divinely motivated joy and happiness, possess every Igbo family, in the name of Jesus. Any place that was given to the devil in any Igbo family, I take you away. Any door that is opened to the devil through house helps, be closed now. I command the spirit of gossip, false prophecy and suspicion to be cast out from every Igbo family, in the name of Jesus. Let the yoke of worldliness and extravagance be broken in Igbo family. Let the yoke of late marriage be broken among Igbo born, in the name of Jesus.

Father Lord, You are the best matchmaker, lead Igbo people into profitable marriages. Let Your plans and purpose for marriage be fulfilled in Igbo land. O Lord, Almighty God, be the one that will bring people together for marriage, in the name of Jesus. Lord Jesus, arise and guide every Igbo person to his or her rightful partner. Every enemy of right choice in marriage, avoid Igbo children. Any unprofitable relationship planned by the devil, be rejected by Igbo persons. O Lord, help Igbo people to make right choices finally, in the name of Jesus.

Let all Igbo bachelors and unmarried women refuse to marry wrong partners. No Igbo child will marry an enemy as a partner, God forbid, in the name of Jesus. O Lord, organize a meeting that will bring people together for true marriages. Let the sons and daughters of Igbo tribe make right choices in marriage. O Lord, make Igbo homes to be heaven on earth. O Lord, bless Igbo women and their men to be the best on earth. O Lord, thank You for keeping watch over the world from creation, in the name of Jesus. Father Lord, arise in Your mercy and protect Igbo land and Igbo people. Let the land of the Igbos and her people be secured by the almighty, in the name of Jesus.

Blessed Holy Trinity, by Your power come and watch over our land. O Lord, arise and silence every evil voice in Igbo land, in the name of Jesus. Let the four corners of Igbo land be protected by God's angels. Every enemy of peace in Igbo land, be exposed and disgraced, in the name of Jesus. O Lord, command Your angels to take over the security of Igbo land. O Lord, arise and fish out every messenger of destruction in Igbo land, in the name of Jesus. Every weapon of the devil in Igbo land, burn to ashes. Blood of Jesus, speak in every place in Igbo land, in the name of Jesus.

Lord Jesus, You are the prince of peace, bring peace in Igbo land. Let the spirit of misunderstanding be cast out from Igbo land, in the name of Jesus. Ancient of days, bring peace in Igbo land as it is in heaven today. Power to live together as brothers and sisters, possess Igbo people. Let the spirit of understanding be released in every place in Igbo land. Any spirit of religion without Christ in Igbo land, be cast out, in the name of Jesus. Let the works of the fresh be destroyed everywhere in Igbo land. Any stranger in Igbo land on a mission to cause trouble, be exposed and disgraced. Blood of Jesus, speak peace in Igbo land at all times, in the name of Jesus. Any evil force ready to cause trouble in Igbo land, be troubled, in the name of Jesus.

DECREES FOR SOLUTION TO EVERY PROBLEM

Every yoke of impossibilities in my life, break to pieces, in the name of Jesus. Any evil hand planting problems into my life, wither by force. Every disease germ in my body, receive death. Father Lord, take me away from the reach of every problem, in the name of Jesus.

Every demonic work going on against my life, stop immediately. Let all the impossibilities in my life disappear now. Any power backing up my problems, withdraw by force, in the name of Jesus.

Any evil pillar supporting my problems, be uprooted. Every enemy of my freedom, wherever you are, be crippled. Blood of Jesus, speak me out of every problem, in the name of Jesus.

You my problems, I confront you with divine solution. Every problem on suicide mission in my life, collapse and quench desperately. Father Lord, solve every problem in my life and empower me with long life, in the mighty name of Jesus.

Let every creature fight and destroy every problem in my life. You my problems, your time is up, expire, in the name of Jesus.

DECREES FOR UNITY IN IGBO NATION

Anointing to love one another, fall upon the Igbos. Let the Spirit of the Almighty bind Igbo people together in love. Harmony from above, come upon the Igbos to the glory of God, in the name of Jesus. Any agent of disunity in Igbo land, be disgraced. Any messenger of conflicts in Igbo land, carry your message to your sender. Let the spirit of misunderstanding in Igbo land be cast out. Heavenly Father, command the unity in heaven to come down upon the Igbos, in the name of Jesus. Any power that is standing on the pathway of Igbo unity, be removed. Any agent of Satan that is opposing the unity of Igbo people, be disgraced, in the name of Jesus.

Let the gods of the land that is fighting against the unity of the Igbos be cast out. Any evil spirit that was imported into Igbo land to scatter them, be cast out. Any angry god that has vowed to scatter the Igbos, be cast out, in the name of Jesus. Let the charity of the Igbos among themselves suffer long. Father Lord, help the Igbos to be kind to one another. Let the spirit of envy in Igbo land that is affecting their unity be destroyed. I command the spirit of pride in any Igbo person to be cast out. Every yoke of disunity in the life of any Igbo person, break, in the name of Jesus.

O Lord, release the spirit of divine agreement among the Igbos. Let practical love begin to manifest in the lives of every Igbo person. Powers to love God and His Word, possess Igbo people. Let the spirit of submission, humility and love for one another possess Igbo people. O Lord, help every Igbo person to be committed for unity among themselves, in the name of Jesus.

DECREES AGAINST ENEMIES OF MY BUSINESS

Ancient of days, command my business to prosper even in the presence of my enemies, in the name of Jesus. I command every enemy raised against my business to expire, in the name of Jesus. Any witchcraft attack against my business, be terminated. Holy Ghost fire, burn to ashes every strange material in my business, in the name of Jesus.

Any evil sacrifice offered against my business; expire. Every door the devil has opened against my business, close forever. Any witchcraft broom prepared against my business, catch fire, in the name of Jesus.

Any evil eye monitoring my business, be blinded now. You my business, disappear from every demonic captivity. Any evil arrest against my business, be terminated, in the name of Jesus.

Every satanic limitation upon my business, disappear. O Lord, arise and move my business out of every enemy's camp, in the name of Jesus

Any power holding my business down, release it and disappear forever, in the name of Jesus. O Lord, deliver my business from my mistakes in life, in the mighty name of Jesus.

DECREES FOR EVERY IGBO PERSON

Lord Jesus, help every Igbo woman to be homely, marriageable and peaceful. O Lord, help the Igbos to invest in their own land, in the name of Jesus. Let companies and industries established anywhere by Igbos prosper. Let Igbo children anywhere in the world be singled out for the best. Every glory that departed out of Igbo land, come back double. Teachers in Igbo land, arise and shine above others in the world, in the name of Jesus. Schools in Igbo land, rise up and become the best in the world, in the name of Jesus. O Lord, bless Igbo sons and daughters and make them masters wherever they are. Let every Igbo person in all parts of the world overcome laziness and challenges, in the name of Jesus.

Father Lord, give every Igbo person a good employment. Let every Igbo person find a means of survival above others. Any civil servant in Igbo land and all over the world, receive grace to prosper. Every trader from Igbo land, rise above others until you get to the top most top. Pastors from Igbo land that are pastoring anywhere in the world, prosper in God's ways above others. O Lord, empower every minister from Igbo land with the gifts of the Holy Ghost. Let the Igbo also produce some of the best scientists in over the world, in the name of Jesus. Let the best professors in every academic department come from the Igbo tribe. O Lord, raise disciplined youths from Igbo land that will rule the world, in the name of Jesus.

Let the lives of Igbo youths positively influence every other youth in the world. O Lord, empower every youth from Igbo tribe to be a standard to others. Power to excel in every good thing, possess the Igbo youths above others. Lord Jesus, release Your power to rise above others into Igbo youths worldwide. Every enemy of Igbo youth, be disgraced without mercy. O Lord, arise and take Igbo youths to their places in life. Almighty God, upgrade the brains of every Igbo student. Let the spirit of understanding capture every Igbo student, in the name of Jesus.

Power for special knowledge, possess every student from Igbo tribe. O Lord, release the best information to every Igbo student by Your power, in the name of Jesus. Every enemy of Igbo student in any part of the world, be disgraced. Let the spirit of first class enter into every Igbo student worldwide. Father Lord, empower every Igbo student worldwide to break academic records. Heavenly Father, deliver every Igbo student from all forms of failure, in the name of Jesus. Power to prevail in all areas of life, possess Igbo students. Lord Jesus, empower every Igbo youth to prevail in sport worldwide. O Lord, make Igbo children the best in any kind of sports, in the name of Jesus.

Anointing to make name in every field of life, possess every Igbo person. O Lord, bring changes in every part of the world that will favor Igbos. Let prevailing darkness against the Igbos be disorganized. Any power that has vowed to cause war in Igbo land by all means, be destroyed, in the name of Jesus. O Lord, assist the Igbos to make it better than the best in the world. Lord Jesus, help the Igbos to unite against her enemies everywhere. O Lord, assist Igbos to make it better than the best in the world. Lord Jesus, help the Igbos to unite against their enemies everywhere. Any weapon of destruction against the Igbos, backfire, in the name of Jesus.

O Lord, empower the Igbos to enter into other nations and assist their community. Let the elders of Igbo land lead other elders aright. Blood of Jesus, preserve great elders in Igbo land to show the way. Let the truth be preserved by Igbo elders worldwide. O Lord, put every Igbo man where they belong in life. Let Igbo chiefs be empowered to preserve the truth and justice. Any idol in Igbo land, be uprooted and destroyed, in the name of Jesus. Let the voice of victory be constant in Igbo land. O Lord, empower our traditional rulers to lead the tribe well, in the name of Jesus.

Let our traditional leaders stand for the truth and fight insecurity. Blood of Jesus, speak every Igbo leader out of idolatry. Let every Igbo occult group in Igbo land be destroyed. Heavenly Father, deliver everyone who need deliverance in

Igbo land. Everlasting God, bring everlasting peace in Igbo land, in the name of Jesus. Let Igbo land be industrialized like no other country in the world. Father Lord, raise great leaders that will help the world from the Igbo tribe. O Lord, empower the Igbos within and outside Nigeria to make name for God, in the name of Jesus.

Blood of Jesus, flow into Igbo land to deliver the land. O Lord, lead Igbo people to the job of their dreams. Father Lord, bless every Igbo person with an establishment that will employ others. Let the business of every Igbo person create wealth and help the nation, in the name of Jesus. Let every single adult in Igbo land become an investor. O Lord, let every Igbo person achieve greatness. Let the wisdom of God possess every Igbo child for greatness. I command every Igbo apprentice to rise above his or her masters, in the name of Jesus.

DECREES FOR FINANCIAL BREAKTHROUGH

Father Lord, issue a fat cheque in my business name that will terminate my financial limits, in the name of Jesus. Blood of Jesus, command finance into my life. Money, what are you waiting for? Appear; come into my life. Power to multiply money through good means; possess me, in the name of Jesus.

You money, begin to look for me, find me and serve me. Power for financial miracle, possess me, left and right. Opportunity to make money in good ways, manifest in my life, in the name of Jesus.

Power to increase in money, in every business, manifest in my life. Every embargo place upon my finances, be lifted by force. Father Lord, link me up with contracts that will bless me financially, in the name of Jesus.

Power to make money in trillions without struggle; possess me. Money, money, money, and how many times have I called you? Rush into my life, in the mighty name of Jesus.

I command every creature to open door for financial breakthrough into my life, in the mighty name of Jesus.

DECREE FOR EVERY IGBO PERSON

Blessed Holy Trinity, I plead with You to get involved in every area of my life. Father Lord, boycott my unworthiness and help me against the rule of law. Let Your mercy be extended to me against every odd, Let Your redemption power, enter into everywhere and set me free. O Lord, command all Your promises to be fulfilled in my life, in the name of Jesus. Blood of Jesus, speak me out of every sin, sickness, troubles and every enemy. Let the grace of God remove all my guilt and let Your mercy terminate my misery, in the name of Jesus.

Father Lord, deliver me from unbelief, reproach and every work of the devil in my life. Let the mercy of God bring salvation, deliverance and give me speed. O Lord, clear all my guilt and give me power over sin. Mercy of God, empower me to do Your will, fulfil my divine purpose on earth and live holy. Blood of Jesus, by Your mercy, speak every evil sacrifice against me to death, in the name of Jesus. O Lord, have mercy on me and protect Your integrity in my life. Father Lord, by Your mercy, do something tangible in my life that will cause people to praise You, in the name of Jesus.

Almighty God, let Your mercy be permanent in my life forever. Mercy of God, take away God's anger, judgment and every problem from me. O Lord, by Your mercy, reverse all the consequences of sin in my life and blot out my transgressions, in the name of Jesus. Let every oppressor of my life be turned away by Your mercy. Mercy of God, position me to fight my battles and overcome my enemies. Let the mercy of God vindicate me, and present me to God for blessings, in the name of Jesus. Father Lord, remember me, hear my prayers and terminate my sufferings. Father Lord, by Your mercy, help me to settle down and establish me in Your will, in the name of Jesus.

Mercy of God, ensure my increase and bless the works of my hands. I receive power and grace to dominate my environment, by Your mercy and grace. Power to fulfill my destiny before I leave this world, possess me, in the name of Jesus. Mercy of God, help me to start everything well and end them in peace. Let the mercy of God secure my protection and give me victory in every battle, in the name of Jesus.

PRAYER MADUEKE'S
TOP 50 BESTSELLING BOOKS

(Click on any of them to view them on Amazon)

1. Speaking Things Into Existence by Faith

2. Praying With the Blood of Jesus

3. The Hidden Supernatural Power in Fasting and Prayer

4. Monitoring Spirits

5. Dictionary of Demons & Complete Deliverance

6. Reversing Satanic Judgments in Heavenly Courts

7. The Reality of Spirit Marriage

8. Defeating the Python Spirit

9. Discerning and Defeating the Ahab & Jezebel Spirit

10. Evil Presence

11. Queen of Heaven

12. Leviathan the Beast

13. Command the Morning, Day and Night

14. Evil Summon

15. 35 Special Dangerous Decrees

16. Releasing Destinies From the Courts of Heaven

17. The Battle Plan For Destroying Foundational Witchcraft

18. Total Destruction and Dominion Over Water Spirits

FREE EBOOKS

In order to say a 'Thank You' for purchasing *School for Igbo Hebrew Nation and Prayer Network*, I offer these books to you in appreciation.

> **Click here or go to madueke.com/free-gift to download the eBooks now** <

CHRISTIAN COUNSELLING

We were created for a greater purpose than only survival and God wants us to live a full life.

If you need prayer or counselling, or if you have any other inquiries, please visit the counselling page on my website madueke.com/counselling to know when I will be available for a phone call.

AN INVITATION TO BECOME A MINISTRY PARTNER

In response to several calls from readers of my books on how to collaborate with this ministry, we are grateful to provide our ministry's bank details.

Be assured that our continued prayers for you will be answered according to God's Word, and as you remain faithful by sowing seeds of faith, God will never forget your labors of love in Christ Jesus.

Send your Seeds to:

In Nigeria & Africa

Bank Name: **Access Bank**

Account Name: **Prayer Emancipation Missions**

Account Number: **0692638220**

In the United States & the rest of the World

Bank Name: **Bank of America**

Account Name: **Roseline C. Madueke**

Account Number: **483079070578**

You can also visit the donation page on my website to donate online: www.madueke.com/donate